$49.90

10638572

PURCELL REMEMBERED

in the same series

DEBUSSY REMEMBERED
edited by Roger Nichols

GERSHWIN REMEMBERED
edited by Edward Jablonski

SATIE REMEMBERED
edited by Robert Orledge

TCHAIKOVSKY REMEMBERED
edited by David Brown

921
Pur

Purcell
Remembered

MICHAEL BURDEN

faber and faber
LONDON · BOSTON

Monastic Library
Holy Cross Monastery
West Park, NY 12493

First published in 1995
by Faber and Faber Limited
3 Queen Square London WC1N 3AU

Phototypeset by Intype, London
Printed in England by Clays Ltd, St Ives plc

© Michael Burden, 1995

Michael Burden is hereby identified as author of this work in accordance with Section 77
of the Copyright, Designs and Patents Act 1988

A CIP record for this book
is available from the British Library

ISBN 0–571–17269–5

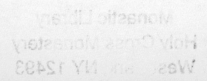
Monastic Library
Holy Cross Monastery
West ... NY 12493

for
Iona

Contents

Illustrations

I am grateful to the following for permission to reproduce photographs: Roxburghe Estates (plate 1), National Portrait Gallery (plates 2, 11), Museum of London (plate 3), The Bodleian Library, Oxford (plates 4, 17), The Ashmolean Museum, Oxford (plates 5, 13), Hulton Deutsch Collection (plates 6, 12), The British Library (plates 7, 8, 14), The Royal Collection © Her Majesty The Queen (plates 9, 10), The Board of the Trustees of the Victoria and Albert Museum (plate 15), The Decca Record Company (plate 16).

Preface

The reader of this volume is, I think, entitled to ask, 'How can we *remember* Purcell?' We are dealing with a period before the establishment of daily newspapers and magazines, and there are no colour supplements to provide a commentary on a day in the life of Henry Purcell or a glimpse of Frances Purcell's sitting-room; nor is there any possibility of oral history, as there has been in other volumes in this series. Much of the information is limited almost exclusively to uninteresting records of payments and other financial matters. There can be no doubt, however, that a picture of Purcell's life may be built up from the scattered sources that we have, and as this volume provides the opportunity to give wider access to material much quoted in part, I have included all the dedications and prefaces to Purcell's published works, bringing them together for the first time.

Purcell Remembered is the brainchild of Helen Sprott, former music editor at Faber and Faber. Her successor, Andrew Clements, kept the project alive, while it was Jane Feaver who, with her usual charm, saw the project through its commissioning stages. Michael Durnin has had the unenviable task of seeing the volume through the press and Ivan Rockey remained conscious during the proof-reading stages.

To the Warden and Fellows of New College, particularly Edward Higginbottom and Martin Williams, and to E. J. Milner-Gulland, I owe the usual but none the less essential day-to-day support. Roger Savage suggested many lines of thought and read the manuscript through, and, as always, Andrew Pinnock has been a fount of knowledge and references. The work of many scholars has been interesting to consult, especially the documentary studies of Franklin B. Zimmerman and Richard Luckett.

A word should be said of my grandmother, the dedicatee of this volume. A descendant of early Australian pioneering families who sailed ketches, mined copper and lived to their hundreds, she has my gratitude for looking upon the frivolous activity of scholarship with benign but appreciative amusement.

Michael Burden
New College, Oxford
1995

Acknowledgements

I am grateful to the following for permission to publish material. Full publication details are given in the endnotes.

Faber and Faber: Constant Lambert, *Music Ho!*; Igor Stravinsky and Robert Craft, *Memories and Commentaries*; Michael Tippett, *Music of the Angels*.

Victor Gollancz: Sidney Buckland (ed.), *Francis Poulenc 'Echo and Source'*.

Oxford University Press: George Dyson, *The Progress of Music*; Donald Francis Tovey, *Essays and Lectures on Music* and *A Musician Talks*; Malcolm Gillies and David Pear (eds.), *The All-Round Man: Selected Letters of Percy Grainger*.

Random House: Claire Harman (ed.), *The Diaries of Sylvia Townsend Warner*.

The Society of Authors on behalf of the Bernard Shaw Estate: Dan H. Laurence (ed.), *Shaw's Music*.

Every effort has been made to contact copyright holders. The publishers would be grateful to be notified of any omissions from the above list.

Chronology

Purcell's Life and Works
Contemporary Figures and Events

It is axiomatic that a selection of events in the arts and in politics is a personal one. All the same, some remarks on this chronology's intentions and its limitations are in order. Political affairs are largely confined to British history. Thus the reader will search in vain for the succession of Popes or the death of foreign monarchs for whom the English court did not go into mourning, but will find a note on the death of Cardinal Mazarin, upon which Louis XIV, who was sympathetic to Charles II's religious and financial difficulties, assumed full government without a first minister. Further, the chronology generally centres on events likely to have impressed themselves on Purcell, so the inauguration of the penny post is mentioned, while the planting of the Champs-Élysées in Paris is not. It would only be fair to acknowledge the many different chronologies I consulted during the preparation of the one that follows; it has to be said, however, that the only thing more surprising than the events their compilers chose to omit were those they decided to include.

1659	*?June* Henry Purcell born, possibly in the Great Almonry in Tothill Street, Westminster; son of Thomas Purcell (d. 1682) or Henry Purcell (d. 1664), later Gentlemen of the Chapel Royal
1659	Thomas Southerne (dramatist) born Richard Cromwell resigns the protectorate; Rump of the Long Parliament recalled in May, dissolved in October and restored in December
1660	Attilio Ariosti, André Campra, Sarah Jennings (later Duchess of Marlborough), Daniel Defoe (novelist), Johann Joseph Fux, George I, Hans Sloane (physician and collector) born Samuel Pepys begins his diary Captain Henry Cooke appointed to a number of posts, including mastership of the Children of the Chapel Royal Royal Society founded First actress appears on an English stage Banking begun by Francis Child Oliver Cromwell's body disinterred and hung on Tyburn gallows Members of parliament who had been excluded in Pride's Purge re-join; the re-formed Long Parliament dissolves itself Charles II and James, Duke of York, return from exile in Holland; land at Dover
1661	Nicholas Hawksmoor (architect) born Peter Lely appointed Court Painter to Charles II William Davenant's *Siege of Rhodes* produced a second time Charles II crowned

Death of Cardinal Mazarin; Louis XIV assumes government
without a first minister

1662   Purcell's brother Daniel probably born (d. 1717); composer of
theatre music
Thomas Purcell appointed composer-in-ordinary for the violins
and to the Private Musick for lutes and voices
Henry Purcell's daughter, Katherine, born

1662   Henry Desmarets born
Henry Lawes (66) dies
Lincoln's Inn Theatre opens under William Davenant's patent
Intelligencer and the *News* begin publication
Royal Society receives its charter
Thomas Killigrew's Drury Lane Theatre granted patent
Robert Boyle discovers the Law of Compatibility (Boyle's Law)
Mary born to James, Duke of York, and Anne Hyde
Charles sells Dunkirk to the French
Revised Book of Common Prayer comes into use
Act of Uniformity passed; Church of England restored
Catherine of Braganza arrives in England, to marry Charles II;
Charles disappointed at her plainness

1663   John Eccles, Tomaso Antonio Vitali born
Thomas Baltzar (*c.* 33), Thomas Selle (64) die
First Drury Lane Theatre opens
Isaac Newton formulates Binomial Theorum
Samuel Cooper appointed His Majesty's Limner
Christopher Wren begins designing the Sheldonian Theatre,
Oxford (finished in 1666)
Charles's waning popularity revived by a royal progress
News of the plague in Amsterdam reaches London

1664   Henry Purcell, possibly Purcell's father, dies

1664   Matthew Prior (poet), John Vanbrugh (dramatist and architect)
born
Christopher Gibbons moves into the Great Almonry
Thomas Willis publishes his *Cerebri anatomi*

1665   Kenelm Digby (writer and diplomat, 62), John Earle (prelate,
tutor and chaplain to Charles II, *c.* 64) die
Nell Gwyn makes her first stage appearance in John Dryden's
Indian Emperour at Drury Lane

First Philosophical Transactions of the Royal Society published
Oxford Gazette (later the *London Gazette*) first published
Second Dutch War begins (to end in 1667)
Plague breaks out in London; Charles leaves Whitehall
Anne born to James and Anne Hyde
Naval Battle of Lowestoft

1666   Michel Pignolet de Montéclair, Jean-Féry Rebel born
Nicholas Lanier (78), James Shirley (dramatist, 70) die
Isaac Newton publishes his Law of Gravitation, and also carries
out experiments with prisms and colons in light
French-trained Louis Grabu sworn in as Master of the King's
Musick
Great Fire of London

1667   'Sweet Tyranness', probably Purcell's first song, published in
John Playford's *Catch that Catch Can*

1667   John Arbuthnot (author), Susannah Centlivre (dramatist),
Antonio Lotti, Johann Christoph Pepusch, Jonathan Swift
(author) born
Johann Jacob Froberger (51), Jeremy Taylor (theologian, 54)
die
Pelham Humfrey returns from France, and becomes Gentleman
of the Chapel Royal
Leadership of the band of twelve violins transferred from John
Banister to Grabu
John Milton publishes *Paradise Lost*; Dryden published *Annus
Mirabilis*
Second Dutch War ends
Lord Clarendon disgraced

1668   Purcell probably becomes a chorister at the Chapel Royal, where
Henry Cooke is Master of the Children

1668   François Couperin born
William Davenant (dramatist and impresario, 62) dies
John Blow appointed organist of Westminster Abbey
Wren appointed surveyor of the City of London
Dryden publishes his essay *Of Dramatic Poesy*; is made Poet
Laureate (remains so until 1688)
Charles II becomes aware of the Duke of York's conversion to
Catholicism

1669   Christopher Simpson (c. 59) dies
        Psyche, a French tragédie-ballet, given at Drury Lane
        Blow appointed musician of the virginals to Charles II
        Pepys closes his diary in fear of blindness
        William Prynne (pamphleteer, author of Histrio-Mastix, 69) dies

1670   Antonio Caldara, William Congreve (dramatist) born
        Cooke is forced to submit an ultimately successful petition on the
        state of the liveries of the boys of the Chapel Royal
        Dryden's and Davenant's version of The Tempest published
        Secret Treaty of Dover signed
        Charter granted to the Hudson Bay Company

1671   Tomaso Giovanni Albinoni, Colley Cibber (dramatist) born
        Anne Hyde, wife of James, Duke of York, and mother of Mary
        and Anne, dies
        Antonio Verrio (artist) comes to England
        Milton's Paradise Regained and Samson Agonistes published
        Dorset Garden Theatre built by William Davenant's widow of
        the Duke's Company
        Wren's monument to the Great Fire begun (finished in 1677)
        Thomas Blood tries to steal the Crown Jewels

1672   Thomas Purcell becomes Marshal of the Corporation of Music
        on Cooke's resignation
        Purcell now taught by Pelham Humfrey, who succeeds Cooke
        as Master of the Children of the Chapel Royal
        Daniel Purcell becomes a chorister of the Chapel Royal

1672   Joseph Addison (writer), Giovanni Bononcini, André Cardinal
        Destouches, Richard Steele (writer) born
        Orazio Benevoli (67), Jacques Champion Chambonnières (c.
        70), Henry Cooke (c. 57), Henrich Schütz (87) die
        The theatre in Drury Lane burns down
        John Banister founds the first concert series in Europe to be
        supported by its box office
        Outbreak of Third Dutch War
        Declaration of Indulgence

1673   Purcell's voice breaks; leaves the choir of the Chapel Royal
        to become assistant to John Hingeston, keeper of the King's
        instruments
        His name first appears in extant records

1673   John Oldmixon (dramatist) born
            Matthew Locke's *Macbeth* and *The Empress of Morocco* performed
            at Dorset Garden
            Wren submits first design for St Paul's Cathedral
            Robert Cambert arrives from France, a victim of Jean-Baptiste
            Lully's political machinations
            Test Act excludes Roman Catholics from office
            James, Duke of York, marries Mary of Modena

1674   Thomas Purcell succeeds John Wilson as musician-in-ordinary
        in the Private Musick
        Blow becomes Purcell's master

1674   ?Jeremiah Clarke, Reinhard Keiser, Beau Nash (master of cere-
            monies) born
            Giacomo Carissimi (69), Pelham Humfrey (27), John Milton
            (poet, 66), John Wilson (79) die
            Blow appointed a Gentleman of the Chapel Royal and Master of
            the Children
            John Evelyn sees an 'Italian opera in Music, the first that had
            been in England'
            Operatic version of *The Tempest* with music by Locke, Pietro
            Reggio, Humfrey and G. B. Draghi performed
            New Drury Lane Theatre opens
            Nicholas Staggins, composer in the Italian style, replaces Grabu
            as Master of the King's Musick
            Cambert, with Grabu, produces his *Ariane, ou Le Mariage de
            Bacchus* at the theatre in Bridges Street under the auspices of the
            Royal Academy of Music, which fails the same year
            Cambert also gives a royal entertainment, including *Pomone*, at
            Windsor
            Third Dutch War ends

1675   Purcell begins his association with Westminster Abbey

1675   James Thornhill (artist and scene designer) born
            Michael Wright (portraitist) paints *John Lay in Three Roles*, one
            of the earliest 'actor pictures'
            Locke's *Psyche* performed at Dorset Garden
            Staggins writes music for the masque of *Calisto* by John Crowne
            given at the Hall Theatre
            First stone of the new St Paul's laid
            Building of the Greenwich Observatory to a design by Wren

	begins; Greenwich Observatory founded
	William Wycherley's *Country Wife* given
1676	Robert Walpole (statesman) born
	Francesco Cavalli (*c.* 74), Christopher Gibbons (*c.* 61), John Greenhill (portraitist, *c.* 32) die
	Godfrey Kneller (portraitist) arrives in London

1677   Composes his first extant anthem, *Lord, who can tell how oft he offendeth?*
Appointed composer-in-ordinary on the death of Locke

1677	Matthew Locke (55) dies
	First performance of *The Rover* by Aphra Behn
	Mary, daughter of James, marries William, Prince of Orange
1678	William Croft, Antonio Vivaldi born
	John Jenkins (86), Andrew Marvell (poet, 57) die
	Thomas Britton's thirty-six-year concert series begins in Clerkenwell Street
	John Banister gives one of the first St Cecilia's Day concerts at the Music School Buildings
	Titus Oates and Israel Tonge appear before the Privy Council to give evidence on the Popish Plot

1679   *Michaelmas* Appointed organist of Westminster Abbey
'What hope for us remains now he is gone?', on the death of Locke

1679	John Banister (54), Thomas Hobbes (philosopher, 91) die
	Charles II dissolves parliament; the Whigs win power; both Houses prorogued
	James retreats to The Hague in the face of mounting anti-Catholicism; returns in October
	Fall of Pepys; resigns secretaryship to the Admiralty and treasurership of Tangier and is sent to the Tower
	Habeas Corpus Act comes into force
	Monmouth defeats the Covenanters at the Battle of Bothwell Bridge

1680   *June-August* Writes nine fantasias
September Marries Frances Peters (d. 1706)
First ode or welcome song, *Welcome, vicegerent of the mighty king*

First definitely attributable music for the theatre: an interpolated
masque and act songs for Nathaniel Lee's *Theodosius*

1680   Emanuele Astorga, Francesco Geminiani born
Samuel Butler (political satirist, 68), Peter Lely (portraitist, 62)
die
Kneller succeeds Lely as Court Painter to Charles II
Proceedings against Pepys dropped
Trial and execution of William Howard, Viscount Stafford
Charles II abandons Catherine of Braganza for the Duchess of
Portsmouth

1681   *July* Purcell's son Henry dies, one week old
Francis Purcell, Thomas's son, appointed groom-in-ordinary to
Charles II
Welcome song for Charles II, *Swifter, Isis, swifter flow*

1681   Georg Philipp Telemann born
William Lilly (astrologer, 79), Gerard Soest (portraitist, *c.* 80)
die
Closterman arrives in England
Shadwell's *Lancashire Witches* performed at Dorset Garden
Charles II prorogues parliament and orders it to reassemble in
Oxford on 21 March; dissolves it shortly after and returns to
Whitehall
Stephen College, the Whig propagandist, executed; Charles
departs for Newmarket
Earl of Shaftesbury tried and acquitted

1682   Moves to St Ann's Lane
July One of the three organists chosen to succeed Edward Lowe
at Westminster Abbey
Thomas Purcell, possibly Purcell's father, dies
August Purcell's son John Baptista baptized; dies two months
later
September His songs appear in the inauguration of William Prit-
chard as Lord Mayor of London
Welcome songs *What shall be done on behalf of the man?* for
James, Duke of York, and *The summer's absence unconcerned we
bear* for Charles II

1682   James Gibbs (architect), John Hadley (mathematician) born

Blow's masque *Venus and Adonis* given at court; Mrs Mary Davis as Venus and Lady Mary Tudor, her daughter by Charles II, as Cupid

Whigs weakened as, with royal interference, the Tory William Pritchard is elected Lord Mayor of London

1683   *February* Eight new songs appear in the fourth book of *Choice Ayres and Songs to Sing*; takes the sacrament in public according to the usage of the Church of England

June Sonnata's of III Parts published

December Seems to become unpaid instrument keeper on Hingeston's death

Ode *From hardly climes and dangerous toils of war* for the marriage of Prince George of Denmark to Princess Anne, welcome song *Fly, bold rebellion* for Charles II and two St Cecilia's Day odes, *Welcome to all the Pleasures* and *Laudate Ceciliam*

1683   George II, Christoph Graupner, Jean-Philippe Rameau born

Thomas Killigrew (dramatist, 71), Izaak Walton (writer and angler, 90) die

'Battle of the Organs' to choose an organ for the Temple Church begins

Duchess of York miscarries of a male heir

Charles II's brother-in-law Alphonso VI, King of Portugal, dies

Penny post established

1684   *November* Thomas Purcell's son Charles sails for Guinea as captain of the sloop the *George*

Welcome song for Charles II, *From those serene and rapturous joys*

1684   François Dagincourt, Jean-François Dandrieu, Francesco Durante, William Kent (architect) born

Johann Rosenmüller (*c.* 65) dies

Organs by Smith (to be played by Blow and Purcell) and by Harris (to be played by Draghi) finished in the Temple Church

Thomas Betterton, with a French company, attempts an opera season at Whitehall

Prince George of Denmark admitted to the Order of the Garter

Whig Rye House Plot to assassinate Charles II

Pepys elected President of the Royal Society

Lighting of London's streets begins

1685   Moves to Bowling Alley East
        February Song on the death of Charles II, *If prayers and tears*
        Provides a second organ for James's coronation
        April Attends coronation as organist of Westminster Abbey; cer-
        emony opens with his *I was glad* and closes with his *My heart is
        inditing*
        August He and thirty-three other musicians appointed musicians-
        in-ordinary – Purcell only as a harpsichordist, not retained as
        composer and organist of the Chapel Royal
        October Welcome song for James II on Monmouth's rebellion,
        Why, why are all the Muses mute?, and probably the St Cecilia's
        Day ode *Raise, raise the voice*

1685   J. S. Bach, John Gay (author), George Frederick Handel,
                Domenico Scarlatti born
                Charles II dies
                French company returns with *Cadmus et Hermione*
                James II crowned; theatres, closed since the death of Charles,
                reopen
                Dryden's *Albion and Albanius*, with music by Grabu, staged at
                Dorset Garden
                St Cecilia's Day ode, Nahum Tate's and William Turner's *Tune
                the viol, touch the lute*, so awful that there was to be no celebration
                in 1686
                Monmouth's rebellion; Earl of Argyll executed for rising in
                support
                Duke of Monmouth executed, after his defeat by James II at the
                Battle of Sedgemoor
                Judge Jeffreys presides over the 'Bloody Assize'; appointed Lord
                Chancellor

1686   *August* Returns from the court at Windsor to bury his son
        Thomas
        September With three other organists, is called to play and judge
        the new organ in St Katherine Cree and to choose an organist
        October Welcome song for James II's birthday, *Ye tuneful Muses*

1686   Benedetto Marcello, Nicola Porpora, Allan Ramsay (poet) born
                Monmouth's defeat marked by Giovanni Battista Vitali's *L'ambi-
                tione debellata overo La caduta di Monmouth* in the Queen's home
                town of Modena

James II goes some way to clearing the musicians' arrears; introduces Catholics into the universities, churches and the Privy Council; suppresses Dryden's *Spanish Fryar*

1687   *June* His son Henry born; dies in August
October Welcome song for James II's birthday, *Sound the trumpet Gentle shepherds, you that know*, on the death of John Playford

1687   Jean Baptiste Senaillé born
Nell Gwyn (actress and mistress of Charles II, *c.* 37), Jean-Baptiste Lully (55), John Playford (64), George Villiers, second Duke of Buckingham (dramatist, 59), Edmund Waller (poet, 81) die
Siface arrives in London, invited by the Queen to join the Chapel Royal
Newton's *Principia* published
Henry Playford's *Harmonia Sacra*, Book I, published
St Cecilia's Day celebration revived with Draghi's *From harmony, from heavenly harmony*, to a text by Dryden
James orders the Fellows of Magdalen College, Oxford, to accept Anthony Farmer, a Catholic, as President
Declaration of Indulgence issued in Scotland allowing Catholics to worship freely, but Quakers and Presbyterians allowed to worship only in private houses

1688   *January* Anthem for the thanksgiving service for the Queen's pregnancy, *Blessed are they that fear the Lord*
November Charles Purcell's estate comes to court

1688   Johann Friedrich Fasch, Prince James (the 'Old Pretender'), Alexander Pope (poet) born
John Bunyan (writer, 60), Francesco Foggia (84) die
Judge Jeffreys finally rules in favour of Smith's organ, played by Blow and Purcell, in the 'Battle of the Organs'
Court musicians ordered by James to play dance music whenever and wherever the Queen's maids required
Henry Playford's first book of *The Banquet of Music* licensed
The Seven Bishops sent to the Tower at the beginning of June for their opposition to the Declaration of Indulgence; acquitted on the 30th
William of Orange accepts an invitation to invade England and lands at Torbay
James goes into exile in France

James Renwick, Scottish Covenanter, executed

1689 *April* Provides a second organ for the coronation; called to relin-
quish the money he had collected from those attending the organ
loft during the ceremony Ode on Mary's birthday, *Now does the
glorious day appear*
July Appointed to the King's Private Musick as 'musician composer'
August Ode at Louis Maidwell's school, *Celestial music*
?August Performance of *Dido and Aeneas* at Josiah Priest's school
in Chelsea

1689   Mary Wortley Montagu (littérateur), Samuel Richardson (novel-
ist) born
Aphra Behn (dramatist and adventurer, 49), Judge Jeffreys (41)
die
By legal fiction, James II's reign ends on 11 February; interreg-
num until William and Mary succeed jointly to the throne on
13 February; crowned at Westminster Abbey in April
Jacobites defeat the royal forces at the Battle of Killicrankie;
Jacobites then defeated at the Battle of Newtown Butler
Bill of Rights introduced

1690 *April* Ode on Mary's birthday, *Arise, my Muse*
First performance of *Dioclesian* at Dorset Garden
Sets as song D'Urfey's ode to the Queen, *High on a throne of
glittering ore* and composes the Yorkshire Feast song, *Of old when
heroes thought it base*

1690   William Babell, Henry Carey, Gottlieb Muffat, Francesco
Maria Veracini, Leonardo Vinci born
Giovanni Legrenzi (*c.* 65) dies
William leaves for Ireland; defeats James at the Battle of the
Boyne
War with France breaks out (to end in 1697)

1691 *April* Ode on Mary's birthday, *Welcome, welcome, glorious morn*
May (probably) First performance of *King Arthur* at Dorset
Garden
June Katherine Purcell marries William Sale

1691   James Quinn (actor) born
Jean-Henri D'Anglebert (56) dies

A band of musicians departs with William for Holland, where he attends the Congress of the Allies at The Hague
Elkanah Settle appointed Poet of London
Surrender of Mons to the French army while William is on his way to lift the siege
Captain Ginkel captures Limerick as William returns from Holland

1692 ?Becomes Master of the Twelve Children
April Ode on Mary's birthday, *Love's goddess sure was blind* given; moves to Marsham Street
May First performance of *The Fairy-Queen* at Dorset Garden
November Performance of ode on St Cecilia's Day, *Hail, bright Cecilia*
December Plays the organ for Mountfort's funeral service

1692 Giuseppe Tartini born
Nathaniel Lee (dramatist, 43), Thomas Shadwell (dramatist, *c.* 50), Giovanni Battista Vitali (*c.* 60) die
Mary suppresses Southerne's and Dryden's *Cleomenes, the Spartan Hero*
Murder of William Mountfort (tragedian, dramatist, singer, 28) and death of Anthony Leigh (comedian) curtail theatrical activity
Nahum Tate appointed Poet Laureate
Gentleman's Journal founded
Scots massacred at Glencoe
William sets off on his campaigns in the Low Countries; Catherine of Braganza departs
Dutch and English fleets defeat the French at La Hogue
Court goes into mourning for the Electress of Bavaria

1693 *April* Ode on Mary's birthday, *Celebrate this festival*
Michaelmas Purcell is paid for teaching the first John Weldon of Eton

1693 Johann Kaspar Kerl (65) dies
William Congreve's first play, *The Old Bachelor*, staged
Henry Playford's *Harmonia Sacra*, Book II, licensed
Entrenchment of the National Debt

1694 *January* Ode on the centenary of Trinity College, Dublin, *Great*

parent, hail, performed
April Ode on Mary's birthday, *Come, ye sons of art, away*
Publication of the twelfth edition of John Playford's *Introduction to the Skill of Musick*, which included Purcell's revisions and canon exemplar

1694   Lord Chesterfield (literary patron and author), Louis-Claude Daquin, Leonardo Leo born
Mary dies of smallpox
Licensing Act expires; effective end to press censorship
Prince of Baden attends a revival of *Dioclesian*
Company of the Bank of England established for the raising of finance for the siege of Namur

1695   *January* Starts to compose music for Mary's funeral
April Richard Busby, teacher of Dryden, Locke and Robert South, dies, leaving Purcell a gold mourning ring
May Daniel Purcell resigns as organist of Magdalen College, Oxford, and moves to London, probably to assist an ailing Henry
July Ode on the birthday of the Duke of Gloucester, *Who can from joy refrain?*
November Purcell dies in London and is buried in Westminster Abbey

1695   Pietro Antonio Locatelli, Giuseppe Sammartini born
Louis Grabu (*c.* 60), William Killigrew (dramatist, 89), Anthony à Wood (antiquary, 63) die
Mary's body lies in state during February and is interred in March
General Boufflers capitulates, Namur falls; William's victory marked by a day of thanksgiving

I

Early life and the Chapel Royal

SAMUEL PEPYS

(1633–1703)

One of the greatest observers of England during the first
years of Henry Purcell's life was the music-loving diarist
Samuel Pepys. The son of a tailor, he was educated at St Paul's
School and Trinity Hall and Magdalene College, Cambridge,
and through the patronage of his father's cousin, the Earl of
Sandwich, ultimately became Secretary to the Admiralty in
1672. He suffered later difficulties, being removed from
office in 1679 for supposed involvement in the Popish Plot,
and again during the 1688 Revolution. The diary covers the
years 1660 to 1669, when he was a resourceful and ambitious
bon vivant. When Purcell was only months old, Charles II
returned from exile. Appropriately, one 'Mr Pursell' –
Thomas, Henry senior or Purcell's uncle, Edward – spent a
celebratory evening with the diarist Samuel Pepys and the
composer Matthew Locke in a coffee-house.

Here I met with Mr. Lock and Pursell, Maisters of Musique; and with
them to the Coffee-house into a room next the Water by ourselfs; where
we spent an hour or two till Captain Taylor came to us, who told us that
the House had voted the gates of the City to be made up again and the
members of the City that are in prison to be let at liberty; and that Sir
G. Booth's case be brought into the House tomorrow.

Here we had variety of brave Italian and Spanish songs and a Canon
for 8 *Voc*:, which Mr. Lock had newly made on these words: *Domine
salvum fac Regem*, an admirable thing.

. . . Here, out of the window it was a most pleasant sight to see the
City from [one] end to the other with a glory about it, so high was the
light of the Bonefires and so thick round the City, and the bells rang
everywhere. Hence home and wrote to my Lord; afterward came down
and found Mr. Hunt (troubled at this change) and Mr. Spong, who
stayed late with me, singing of a song or two, and so parted. My wife
not very well, went to bed before.[1]

It was clearly essential that the court should recover its former
style and grandeur as quickly as possible to restore the confidence of the people. Indeed, such was the haste to have

music re-established as part of this revival that in the Lord
Chamberlain's accounts the first entry after the Restoration is
a note for the appointment of Henry Cooke (*c.* 1615–1672)
as a bass in the King's Private Musick.

Henry Cooke had been a member of the Chapel Royal
before the Commonwealth and had fought for the royalists
during the Civil War, attaining the rank of captain. One of
the royal posts to which he was appointed in 1660 was the
mastership of the Children of the Chapel Royal, on 29 September. Despite the inclusion among the newly sworn Gentlemen of those who had been members of the Chapel Royal
before the Commonwealth, it comes as no surprise to find
that the interregnum seriously affected the quality of the
choir's performances. As Pepys wrote on 14 October 1660:

Lords day. early to my Lord's, in my way meeting with Dr. Fairebrother,
who walked with me to my father's back again; and there we drank our
morning draught, my father being gone to church and my mother asleep
in bed. Here he caused me to put my hand, among a great many
Honourable hands, to a paper or Certificate on his behalfe.

To White-hall Chappell, where one Dr Crofts made an indifferent
sermon and after it an anthemne, ill sung, which made the King laugh.
Here I first did see the Princesse Royall since she came into England.
Here I also observed how the Duke of Yorke and Mrs. Palmer did talke
to one another very wantonly through the hangings that parts the King's
closet and the closet where the ladies sit.[2]

Cooke seems to have worked hard and fast, for in February
1661 Pepys was able to note:

After dinner to White-hall chappell with Mr. Childe; and there did hear
Captain Cooke and his boy make a tryall of an Anthemne against tomorrow, which was rare Musique.[3]

Although Pepys appreciated Cooke's qualities, he did not
always report with equal enthusiasm on Cooke's compositions
and on his character. His later encounter with the Master of
the Children conveys an impatience with Cooke's undoubted
self-importance.

After dinner, Captain Cooke and two of his boys to sing; but it was
endeed, both in performance and composition, most plainly below what

I heard last night, which I could not have believed. Besides, overlooking the words when he sung, I find them not at all humourd as they ought to be, and as I believed he had done all he had set – though he himself doth endeed sing in a manner, as to voice and manner, the best I ever heard yet; and a strange mastery he hath in making of extraordinary surprizing closes, that are mighty pretty; but his bragging that he doth understand tones and sounds as well as any man in the world, and better then Sir W. Davenant or anybody else, I do not like by no means; but was sick of it and him for it.[4]

> The Children of the Chapel Royal received liveries, and warrants for their provision at various times can be found throughout the records of the period. The most detailed gives a picture of the style of livery Purcell would have worn when entering the Chapel Royal in the late 1660s.

Warrant to deliver to Henry Cooke, master of the twelve children of the Chappell Royall, the following materials for their liveries: For each of them one cloak of bastard cloth lyned with velvett, one suit and coat of the same cloth made up and trimmed with silver and silk lace after the manner of our footmen's liveries, and also to the said suit, three shirts, three half shirts, three pair of shoes, three pair of thigh stockings, whereof one pair of silk and two pairs of worsted, two hats with bands, six bands and six pairs of cuffs, whereof two laced and four plain, three handkerchiefs, three pairs of gloves and two pieces and a half of rebon for trimming garters and shoestrings. And at Easter for their summer liveries, for each boy one cloak of bastard scarlett lined with sattin and one doublet of sattin with bastard scarlett trunk hose made and trimmed up as aforesaid, with three shirts, three half shirts, three pairs of shoes, three pairs of thigh stockings, whereof one pair of silk and two pairs of worsted, two hats with bands etc.[5]

> The Chapel Royal was gradually coming to life. And there was more. At the chapel at Whitehall, the seat of the Chapel Royal for much of Purcell's lifetime, we find, among other things, the instructions for building a new organ loft and attendant rooms in 1663:

LC to Surveyor General. Warrant to make and erect a large organ loft by his Maties Chappell at Whitehall, in the place where formerly the great

Double organ stood, and to rebuild the roomes over the bellowes roome, two stories high, as it was formerly, the lower story for the subdean of his Maties Chappell, and the upper story with two rooms, one of them for the organist in wayting and the other for the keeper and repayrer of his Maties organs, harpsicords, virginalls, and other Instruments, each room to have a Chymney, and Boxes and shelves for keeping the materials as belonging to the organ, and the organ books.[6]

> These were the rooms Purcell was to inhabit when, on leaving the choir in 1673, he was appointed assistant to John Hingeston, keeper of the King's keyboard and wind instruments.

> Purcell can hardly have remained in ignorance of the two great calamities of the Restoration, the plague of 1665 and the Great Fire of 1666. Henry Purcell senior, who may have been his father, was dead by 1664, thought by some to have succumbed to an early outbreak of the plague in Westminster. In April 1665 Pepys wrote:

Great fears of the Sickenesse here in the City, it being said that two or three houses are already shut up. God preserve us all.[7]

> Pepys records the spread of the main outbreak in London and its environs, noting its arrival in Westminster near the Purcell family in 1665, even as it seemed to be over in the City.

This day I informed myself that there died four or five at Westminster of the plague, in one alley in several houses upon Sunday last – Bell Alley, over against the Palace-gate. Yet people do think that the number will be fewer in the town then it was the last week.[8]

> Pepys gives many glimpses and much detail of the activity in the City, but the most evocative and spine-chilling is his discovery of a corpse in August.

It was dark before I could get home; and so land at church-yard-stairs, where to my great trouble I met a dead Corps, of the plague, in the narrow ally, just bringing down a little pair of stairs – but I thank God I was not much disturbed at it. However, I shall beware of being late abroad again.[9]

> The plague was virtually over by the end of November 1665, though there were outbreaks without London and Westmins-

ter during the following year. Despite the trauma that the
population had suffered, however, the celebrations seem to
have been perfunctory at best.

I to the office a little, and then to church, it being Thanksgiving day for
the cessation of the plague. But Lord, how the town doth say that it is
hastened before the plague is quite over, there dying some people still,
but only to get ground of Plays to be publicly acted, which the Bishops
would not suffer till the plague was over. And one would think so, by
the suddenness of the notice given of the day, which was last Sunday, and
the little ceremony: the sermon being dull, of Mr Milles, and people
with great indifferency came to hear him.[10]

> As if the plague were not enough, the much tried capital was
> swept by a fire which laid waste approximately four fifths of
> the City and destroyed many landmarks, including St Paul's
> Cathedral and Gresham's Royal Exchange. Pepys gives a
> description of the blaze, conveying clearly what must have
> been seen by the Purcell family in Westminster.

Only, now and then walking into the garden and saw how horridly the
sky looks, all on a fire in the night, was enough to put us out of our wits;
and endeed it was extremely dreadfull – for it looks just as if it was at
us, and the whole heaven on fire.[11]

> Pepys goes on:

I after supper walked in the dark down to Tower-street, and there saw it
all on fire at the Trinity house on that side and the Dolphin tavern on
this side, which was very near us – and the fire with extraordinary
vehemence. Now begins the practice of blowing up of houses in Tower-
street, those next the Tower, which at first did frighten people more then
anything; but it stop[ped] the fire where it was done.[12]

> Even during the height of the conflagration Pepys, indefatig-
> ably chronicling events, found time to observe the value
> placed by the populace on their musical instruments.

Good hopes there was of stopping it at the Three Cranes above, and at
Buttolphs-Wharf below bridge, if care be used; but the wind carries it
into the City, so as we know not by the water-side what it doth there.
River full of lighter[s] and boats taking in goods, and good goods

swimming in the water; and only, I observed that hardly one lighter or boat in three that had the goods of a house in, but there was a pair of virginalls in it.[13]

> Pepys, no doubt like other Londoners, was afterwards to dream of the fire on several occasions.
>
> Later that year he gives us what is possibly the first glimpse of Purcell's musical activities. In an effort to escape the company of Samuel Atkins – 'the fellow I hate, and so I think all the world else do' – after an unprofitable financial discussion on 23 November 1666 Pepys took him in a carriage to the Temple,

and he being gone, with all the haste back again and to my chamber late, to enter all this day's matter of accounts in my book.[14]

> Pepys clearly paused for a while, though, and behind the retreating back of the despised Atkins

called at Playfords and there find that his new impression of his Ketches are not yet out, the fire having hindered it; but his man tells me that it will be a very fine piece – many things new being added to it.[15]

> The publisher's note tells us, as John Playford probably did Pepys:

THIS Book had been much sooner abroad, had not the late sad Calamities retarded both Printer and Publisher.[16]

> Among the 'many things new' added to the volume, entitled *Catch that Catch Can, or The Musical Companion*, was 'Sweet Tyranness', generally considered to be Purcell's first composition. Playford dedicated the collection *'To his endeared Friends of the late* Musick-Society *and* Meeting, *in the* Old-Jury, London' who had already given *'Excellent Musical performances, when it was thrown before you in loose Papers'*.
>
> Pelham Humfrey (1647–74), who had become a chrorister by the end of 1660 and a Gentleman of the Chapel Royal in 1667, succeeded Cooke as Master of the boys in 1672, and can probably be counted one of Purcell's early teachers. His skill as a composer had been noted earlier by Pepys, who on attending a morning service in November 1663, commented on Humfrey's anthem *Have mercy upon me, O God*:

the Anthemne was good after sermon, being the 51 psalme – made for five voices by one of Captain Cookes boys, a pretty boy – and they say there are four or five of them that can do as much. And here I first perceived that the King is a little Musicall, and kept good time with his hand all along the Anthem.[17]

> The irritating behaviour of the King, observed drily by Pepys, is attested to by Roger North, for the nobility, aping their monarch, had caused it to become a widespread habit.
>
> After his early years in the Chapel Royal Humfrey had gone to France and to Italy, doubtless encountering musicians and composers, as well as a range of foreign musical styles. Pepys heard some of the fruits of this journey in 1667, though the provision, in the French manner, of 'symphonys' between the verses of the anthem displeased him:

and so I to the Chapel and there stayed (it being Allhollows day) and heard a fine Anthemne, made by Pellam (who is come over) in France, of which there was great expectation; and endeed is a very good piece of Musique, but still I cannot call the Anthem anything but Instrumentall music with the Voice, for nothing is made of the words at all.[18]

> Pepys was displeased not only by the symphonies, but also by Humfrey's manner and style, graphically caught in a famous passage penned later that month:

there [at home] find, as I expected, Mr. Cæsar and little Pellam Hum-phrys, lately returned from France and is an absolute Monsieur, as full of form and confidence and vanity, and disparages everything and everybody's skill but his own. The truth is, everybody says he is very able; but to hear how he laughs at all the King's music here, as Blagrave and others, that they cannot keep time nor tune nor understand anything, and that Grebus the Frenchman, the King's Master of the Musique, how he understands nothing nor can play on any instrument and so cannot compose, and that he will give him a lift out of his place, and that he and the King are mighty great, and that he hath already spoke to the King of Grebus, would make a man piss. I had a good dinner for them, as a venison pasty and some fowl, and after dinner we did play, he on the Theorbo, Mr. Cæsar on his French lute, and I on the viol, but made but mean music; nor do I see that this Frenchman doth so much wonders

on the Theorbo, but without question he is a good musician; but his
vanity doth offend me.[19]

> What the comparatively down-to-earth Purcell made of the
> new Master of the Children on his appointment in 1672,
> shortly before Purcell's voice broke, sadly remains
> unrecorded. Throughout this period a large number of famil-
> ies took part in private music-making of one kind or another,
> and the musical Purcells can have been no exception. Pepys,
> a talented amateur and the possessor of a sharp ear, describes
> many private performances – and, indeed, many casual public
> ones – in which he participated or which he simply observed.
> Several facets of Restoration musical life are touched on in a
> diary entry of 1663.

By and by, about 7 or 8 a-clock, homeward; and changing my horse
again, I rode home, coaches going in great crowd to the further end of
the town almost. In my way in Leadenhall-street there was morris dancing,
which I have not seen a great while. So set up my horse at Games's,
paying 5s for him, and so home to see Sir J Minnes, who is well again;
and after staying talking with him a while, I took leave and went to hear
Mrs. Turner's daughter (at whose house Sir J. Mennes lies) play on the
Harpsicon; but Lord, it was enough to make any man sick to hear her;
yet was I forced to commend her highly.

So home to supper and to bed, Ashwell playing upon the Tryangle
very well before I went to bed.[20]

> The King continued to interest himself in the conduct of
> music at court, music-making in which the Purcell family
> was involved. Charles's penchant for things French led to
> discord among the players, though some of his actions were
> probably inspired by the difficulties of which Humfrey com-
> plained. The directorship of the '24 Violins' engendered much
> comment, which reached Pepys's ears.

Here they talk also how the King's viallin, Bannister, is mad that the
King hath a Frenchman come to be chief of some part of the King's music
– at which the Duke of York made great mirth.[21]

> Court gossip aside, Charles's reign gave the country, out-
> wardly at least, some stability; it survived a number of early
> conspiracies, helped by the exercising of strict laws against

dissenters and nonconformists. With regard to the succession on which such stability relied, his marriage to Catherine of Braganza was childless; his liaisons, however, were not. The most famous of these – that with the actress Eleanor Gwyn – was the subject of much ribald comment and many scurrilous verses.

> Hard by Pall Mall lives a wench call'd Nell.
>   King Charles the Second he kept her.
> She hath got a trick to handle his p—,
>   But never lays hands on his sceptre.
> All matters of state for her soul she does hate,
>   And leave to the politic bitches.
> The whore's in the right, for 'tis her delight
>   To be something just where it itches.[22]

The lack of an heir was a cause of great public disquiet, particularly after Charles's brother, James, openly avowed his Catholicism and married the Catholic Mary of Modena in 1673. Further, unbeknownst to the public and to parliament, Charles had signed the Treaty of Dover in 1670, a document in which he formed a secret alliance with Louis XIV of France. The terms of the treaty – that Charles and James agreed to join the Catholic Church and enter into an alliance with France against Holland in exchange for the payment to Charles of £200,000 per annum – left the future of the country far from certain.

II

Singers, singing and
a celebration of music

Towards the end of 1673 Purcell's years as one of the Children of the Chapel Royal came to an end when his voice broke, at a then early age. Like other choristers, he received a pay-off in the form of clothing, record of which is found in the warrants issued by the Lord Chamberlain.

Clothes for a Chapel boy whose voice is changed. These are to signify unto you His Majesty's pleasure, that you provide and deliver, or cause to be delivered, unto Henry Purcell, late one of the Children of His Majesty's Chapel Royal, whose voice is changed and is gone from the Chapel, two suits of plain cloth, two hats and hat-bands, four whole shirts, four half shirts, six bands, six pair of cuffs, six handkerchiefs, four pair of stockings, four pair of shoes, and four pair of gloves.[1]

Bill for handkerchiefs for Pursell a boy gone from the chapel.[2]

The warrants also show that, unusually, he had other financial help.

Warrant to pay Henry Purcell, late of the Children of His Majesty's Chapell Royall, whose voice is changed and gon from the Chapell, the sum of £30 by the year, to commence Michaelmas, 1673, last past.[3]

And, further, that he was given employment in the form of an assistantship to John Hingeston, a post that he would officially hold until the older man's death in December 1683.

Warrant to swear and admit Henry Purcell in the place of keeper, mender, maker, repairer and tuner of the regals, organs, virginals, flutes and recorders, and all other kinds of wind instruments whatsoever, in ordinary, without fee, to His Majesty, and assistant to John Hingston, and upon the death or other avoidance of the latter, to come in ordinary with fee.[4]

Some idea of the range of duties Purcell must have undertaken

is given in the Lord Chamberlain's warrant below, ordering
the Treasurer of the Chamber

to pay £83. 15s. to John Hingston, keeper and repairer of his Majesty's
organs, for taking down the organ in her Majesty's Chapel at St. James's,
and re-mounting the same in the new music room; for mending the organs
and harpsichords; also for mending her Majesty's harpsichord that stands
in her own chamber; for mending a 'claricon'; for erecting an organ in
the Banquetting House at Whitehall against Maundy Thursday, and for
diverse other things.[5]

MATTHEW LOCKE
(c. 1621–1677)

As well as working for Hingeston, Purcell appears to have
kept in close touch with the Catholic composer and writer on
music Matthew Locke. Locke was responsible for some of
the music to what was probably the first English opera, *The
Siege of Rhodes* (1656), contributions to the masque *Cupid and
Death* (1653) and *The Mask of Orpheus* in Elkanah Settle's
Empress of Morocco (1673). His pamphleteering was less
inventive; it was also vitriolic and shows a marked reluctance
to engage in any meaningful debate. The original of a letter
Locke wrote to Henry Purcell (possibly around 1676) cannot
be traced and the existing copy may be a forgery; nevertheless,
the picture of private rehearsal and music-making it evokes
is one borne out by other sources.

DEAR HARRY,
Some of the gentlemen of His Majesties Musick will honor my poor
lodgings with their company this evening, and I would have you come
and join them: bring with thee, Harry, thy last anthem, and also the
canon we tried over together at our last meeting. Thine in all kindness,
M. Locke.
Savoy, March 16[6]

JOHN GOSTLING
(c. 1650–1733)

The English singer and music copyist John Gostling, who was reputed to have possessed a deep bass voice, had a variety of ecclesiastical appointments from 1674 until his death in 1733; from 1679 he was also a Gentleman of the Chapel Royal. We have almost no record of Purcell's relationship with his singers. One of the few documented accounts of Purcell's writing something at a singer's request is the anthem *They that go down to the sea in ships*. John Hawkins (1719–89) gives us the following description of the circumstances behind the commission; it is perhaps poetic justice that Charles II did not live long enough to hear it.

The King had given orders for building a yacht, which, as soon as it was finished, he named the Fubbs, in honour of the Duchess of Portsmouth, who we may suppose was in her person rather full and plump. The sculptors and painters apply this epithet to children, and say, for instance of the boys of Fiammengo, that they are fubby. Soon after the vessel was launched the king made a party to sail in this yacht down the river, and round the Kentish coast; and, to keep up the mirth and good humour of the company, Mr. Gostling was requested to be of the number. They had got as low as the North Foreland, when a violent storm arose in which the king and the duke of York were necessitated, in order to preserve the vessel, to hand the sails and work like common seamen; by good providence however they escaped to land: but the distress they were in made an impression on the mind of Mr. Gostling, which was never effaced. Struck with a just sense of the deliverance, and the horror of the scene which he had but lately viewed, upon his return to London he selected from the psalms those passages which declare the wonders and terrors of the deep and gave them to Purcell to compose as an anthem, which he did, adapting it so peculiarly to the compass of Mr. Gostling's voice, which was a deep bass, that hardly any person but himself was then, or has since, been able to sing it; but the king did not live to hear it.[7]

APHRA BEHN

(1640–89)

Purcell's own voice type is unknown; his place among the basses at the coronation of James II is, however, suggestive, and it seems that he was heard by Aphra Behn. Perhaps the first professional woman writer in England, Behn was a colourful character. She visited Surinam (perhaps meeting the enslaved Negro 'Prince Oroonoko'), and spied for the British government in Antwerp. How, when and where she heard Purcell – assuming 'Mr. P.' is he – remains obscure; her powerful pindaric ode on her reluctant enslavement to his voice appeared in 1685.

A PINDARIC to Mr. P. who sings finely.
By Mrs. *A. B.*

Damon, altho you waste in vain,
    That pretious breath of thine,
Where lies a Pow'r in every strain,
    To take in any other heart, but mine;
Yet do not cease to sing, that I may know,
    By what soft Charms and Arts,
What more than Humane 'tis you do,
    To take, and keep your hearts;
Or have you Vow'd never to wast your breath,
    But when some Maid must fall a Sacrifice,
As *Indian* Priests prepare a death,
    For Slaves t'addorn their Victories,
Your Charm's as powerful, if I live,
    For I as sensible shall be,
What wound you can, to all that hear you, give,
    As if you wounded me;
And shall as much adore your wondrous skill,
As if my heart each dying Note cou'd kill.

And yet I should not tempt my Fate,
    Nor trust my feeble strength,

Which does with ev'ry softening Note abate
    And may at length
Reduce me to the wretched Slave I hate;
'Tis strange extremity in me,
To venture on a doubtful Victory,
Where if you fail, I gain no more,
Than what I had before;
But 'twill certain comfort bring,
    If I unconquer'd do escape from you;
If I can live, and hear you sing,
No other Forces can my Soul subdue;
Sing, *Damon*, then, and let each Shade,
Which with thy Heavenly voice is happy made,
Bear witness if my courage be not great,
To hear thee sing, and made a safe retreat.[8]

SAMUEL TAYLOR COLERIDGE
(1772–1834)

It was not only poets contemporary with Purcell who were
inspired by hearing his music sung. In 1800 the English
poet Samuel Taylor Coleridge, having heard William Linley
perform one of Purcell's songs, penned the following lines
on death. Coleridge was closely associated with Robert Southey, with whom he shared Romantic and revolutionary views;
his later connection with William and Dorothy Wordsworth
resulted in the publication of *Lyrical Ballads* (1798), a volume
which opened with Coleridge's *Rime of the Ancient Mariner*
and closed with Wordsworth's *Lines Written a few Miles Above
Tintern Abbey*.

LINES TO W. LINLEY, ESQ.
While he sang a song to Purcell's music

While my young cheek retains its healthful hues,
And I have many friends who hold me dear;
L———! methinks, I would not often hear
Such melodies as thine, lest I should lose

All memory of the wrongs and sore distress
For w'ich my miserable brethren weep!
But should uncomforted misfortunes steep
My daily bread in tears and bitterness;
And if at death's dread moment I should lie
With no beloved face by my bed-side,
To fix the last glance of my closing eye,
O God! such strains breath'd by my angel guide,
Would make me pass the cup of anguish by,
Mix with the blest, nor know that I had died![9]

PIERRE MOTTEUX
(1660–1718)

The journalist Pierre Motteux gave an account of the St
Cecilia's Day celebrations that took place in London during
the seventeenth century, for which Purcell was to produce
some of his finest ode settings. They were annual events from
about 1683, and had varying success. Motteux was writing
in October 1692, one month in advance of the forthcoming
celebrations.

THE 22[d] of *November*, being St. *Cœcilia's* day, is observ'd through all
Europe by the Lovers of Music. In *Italy*, *Germany*, *France*, and other
Countries, Prizes are distributed on that day in some of the most consider-
able Towns to such as make the best Anthem in her praise. She was a
Roman Lady of the Noble Family of the *Cœcilii*, from whence the *Cecils* in
England are said to be descended. She is recorded to have been a Lady of an
eminent Beauty and Piety, and a Lover of Music, having suffered Martyr-
dom for the Christian Faith, for which she hath a place allowed her by the
Church of *Rome* in the Calendar. If you will believe their Legends, she
had espoused a fine Gentleman, and lived with him till his death, yet
remained a Virgin; and refusing to sacrifice to the Gods, was shut up in one
of the Baths in her own house being empty, and without water; and tho a
great Fire was made under it for a day and a night, yet far from receiving
hurt by it, it seemed to her a place of pleasure and refreshing, which one
Almachius seeing, he order'd her head to be cut off in that place. They add,
that the Hangman gave her three Blows, yet did not cut off her head

altogether, but left it even as it was hanging by the skin, and that she lived three days thus wounded, comforting those that came to see her. This *Alfonso Villegas*, a *Spanish* Compiler of *Legends*, whose Book is printed with an Approbation of the Divines of *Doway*, relates. Tho the last of these Miracles must seem but small to those who have read of St. *Denys* carrying his head in his hands three or four Miles; and St. *Patrick's* swimming with his in his Teeth: that about her Husband will doubtless be called in question. On that day or the next when it falls on a *Sunday*, as it did last time, most of the Lovers of Music, whereof many are persons of the first Rank, meet at *Stationers-Hall* in *London*, not thro a Principle of Superstition, but to propagate the advancement of that divine Science. A splendid Entertainment is provided, and before it is always a performance of Music by the best Voices and Hands in Town; the Words, which are always in the Patronesses praise, are set by some of the greatest Masters in Town. This year [1691] Dr. *John Blow*, that famous Musician, composed the Music, and Mr. *Durfey*, whose skill in things of that nature is well enough known, made the Words, 6 Stewards are chosen for each ensuing year, four of which are either Persons of Quality or Gentlemen of Note, and the two last, either Gentlemen of their Majesties Music, or some of the chief Masters in Town: Those for that last Year were, the Honourable *James Saunderson* Esq; Sir *Frances Head* Baronet, Sir *Thomas Samwel* Baronet, *Charles Blunt* Esq, Mr. *John Goodwin*, and Mr. *Robert Carr*: and those chosen for the next, Sir *Thomas Travel*, Bar. *Josias Ent*, Esq; Sir *Charles Carteret*, Bar. *John Jeffrys* Esq; *Henry Hazard*, Esq; and Mr. *Barkhurst*. This Feast is one of the genteelest in the world; there are no formalities nor gatherings like as at others, and the appearance is always very splendid. Whilst the Company is at Table, the Hautboys and Trumpets play successively. Mr. *Showers* hath taught the latter of late years to sound with all the softness imaginable, they plaid us some flat Tunes, made by Mr. *Finger*, with a general applause, it being a thing formerly thought impossible upon an Instrument design'd for a sharp key.[10]

> Purcell's first contribution to this annual celebration was a setting of Christopher Fishburn's text 'Welcome to all the Pleasures', performed in 1683 at what may have been the first in the series of seventeenth-century St Cecilia's Day feasts. When the piece was published the following year, Purcell dedicated it to the officers of 1683.

To the Gentlemen of the Musical Society, and particularly the Stewards for the year ensuing, William Bridgman, Esq.; Nicholas Staggins, Doctor in Music; Gilbert Dolben, Esq.; and Mr. Francis Forcer.

Gentlemen, Your kind approbation and benign reception of the performance of these musical compositions on St. Cecilia's Day (by way of gratitude) claim this dedication; which likewise furnishes the author with the opportunity of letting the world know the obligations he lies under to you; and that he is to all lovers of music, a real friend and servant, HENRY PURCELL.[11]

> Also for the 1684 feast, though not necessarily for the same occasion, Purcell appears to have composed the small ode *Laudate Ceciliam*; his other Cecilian odes include *Raise, raise the voice* – and the magnificent *Hail, bright Cecilia*, which was performed in 1692. Motteux gives a brief description of that year's celebrations.

In my first Journal I gave you a large account of the Musick Feast on St. *Cecilia's* day; So, to avoid repetitions, I shall onely tell you that the last was no ways inferiour to the former . . . The following Ode was admirably set to Music by Mr. *Henry Purcell*, and perform'd twice with universal applause, particularly the second Stanza, which was sung with incredible Graces by Mr. *Purcell* himself.[12]

> Motteux, of course, is ambiguous: did Purcell perform the graces or simply compose them? That he believed graces came naturally to a competent musician is illustrated by one of the few anecdotes of the composer that has come down to us. About this time Purcell encountered the prodigious talent of Jemmy Bowen, whose musical prowess was compared by Anthony Aston to Jack Verbruggen's style of acting. When Bowen was

practising a Song set by Mr. PURCELL, some of the Music told him [Bowen] to grace and run a Division in such a Place. *O let him alone*, said Mr. *Purcell*; *he will grace it more naturally than you, or I, can teach him*.[13]

> The song is unidentifiable, but it is thought that he sang at least for Queen Mary's birthday ode in 1693, and in the music that Purcell composed for *Abdelazer* in 1695.

CHRISTOPHER SMART

(1722–71)

Purcell and St Cecilia come together in Christopher Smart's long *Ode for Musick on St Cecilia's Day*. Smart, a poet and fellow of Pembroke College, Cambridge, was troubled by an imprudent marriage and an inability to handle money; in 1747 he was confined to his rooms by creditors. His subsequent career took him to London, where he made an uncertain living as a 'bookseller's hack'. Dogged by melancholia, he died insane in 1771.

From
Ode for Musick on St Cecilia's Day

But hark! the Temple's hollow'd Roof resounds,
And *Purcell* lives among the solemn sounds –
  Mellifluous, yet manly too,
   He pours his strains along,
  As from the lyon Sampson slew,
   Comes sweetness from the strong
  Not like the soft *Italian* swains,
   He trills the weak enervate strains,
    Where sense and musick are at strife;
  His vigorous notes with meaning teem,
   With fire, with force explain the theme,
    And sing the subject into life.
Attend – he sings *Cecilia* – matchless Dame!
 'Tis She – 'tis She – fond to extend her fame,
On the loud chords the notes conspire to stay,
And sweetly swell onto a long delay.
   And dwell delighted on her name.
  Blow on, ye sacred organs, blow,
  In tones magnificently slow;
  Such is the musick, such as the lays,
  Which suit your fair Inventress' praise:
  While round religious silence reigns,
  And loitering winds expect the strains.

Hail majestic mournful measure
Source of many a pensive pleasure!
Best pledge of love to mortals giv'n,
As pattern of the rest of heav'n!
And thou chief honour of the veil,
Hail, harmonious Virgin, hail!
When *Death* shall blot out every name,
And *Time* shall break the trump of Fame,
Angels may listen to thy lute;
Thy pow'r shall last, thy bays shall bloom,
When tongues shall cease, and worlds consume,
And all the tuneful spheres be mute.[14]

JOHN HAWKINS AND THE CATCH

This is all very grandiose stuff, but Purcell did not restrict his composing or singing activities to such exalted circumstances. Some time was clearly spent at the local tavern or at the coffee-house, where the singing of catches and glees was a communal activity, as John Playford's 1667 dedication to *Catch that Catch Can* suggests.

To his endeared Friends of the late Musick-Society *and* Meeting, *in the* Old-Jury, London.

Charles Pigon *Esq*;
Mr. Tho. Tempest *Gent*.
Mr. Herbert Pelham *Gent*.
Mr. John Pelling *Citizen*.

Mr. Benjamin Walington *Citizen*.
Mr. George Piggot *Gent*.
Mr. Francis Piggot *Citizen*.
Mr. John Rogers *Gent*.

SIRS,

Having taken the pains to bring this Musical-Companion *into the World, I knew not where it would find better Entertainment then under your protection, having already given very great Testimony thereof, by your Excellent Musical performances, when it was thrown before you in loose Papers; which makes me not to question the Welcome it will now receive coming to your hand so entire in one Volume with all its Parts. And I doubt not but as most of you have ingenuously acknowledged, that you have gained much benefit by my former labours in this admired Science of Musick; so you and others will now by this so well stored* Companion of Musick *reap both Pleasure and Delight, which is the sole end and desire of*

Your Servant and Well-wisher

John Playford

Philo-Musicae.[15]

Not all purchasers of the volume understood what Playford intended, however, and the next edition contained the following instructions, as well as some interesting comments on the way in which catches were viewed by the seventeenth-century musical snob.

Advertisement relating to the First Book

I Thought it necessary for Information of some Songsters who are not well acquainted with the Nature and Manner of Singing Catches, to give them these Directions: First, a Catch is a Song for three Voyces, wherein the several Parts are included in one; or, as it is usually tearmed, Three Parts in One. Secondly, The Manner of Singing them is thus, The First begins and Sings the Catch forward, and when he is at that Note over which this [:S:] Mark or Signature is placed, the Second begins and Sings forward in a like manner, and when he is Singing that Note over which the said Signature is, the Third begins and Sings, following the other, each Singing it round two or three times over, and so conclude.

This kind of *Musick* hath for many Years past been had in much estimation by the most Judicious and Skiful Professors of *Musick*, for the Excellency of the Composition and Pleasant Harmony; and no late *Musick* that I have met with affords so much Delightful Recreation, though some fond Ignorant Novices in *Musick* have Cry'd them down, because the height of their Skill is not able to understand them. But being unwilling so much good *Musick* should be buried in oblivion, it has made me adventure them once more into the World, for the benefit of future Ages: And I am sure they will be welcome at this time to many Judicious Persons, to whom I recommend them; For this is a Catching Age, all kinds of Catches and Catchers are abroad, *Catch that Catch Can*, *Catch that Catch may*, *Thine Catch it, and mine Catch it*; But these harmless *Catches* my wish is, those that Catch them with delight to Learn and for Instruction, may hereby reap both Pleasure and Delight: But those that Catch at them with detraction (as that is a Catching disease) may Catch only the First of their own Envy and Malice. But to conclude, Take the Commendatory Lines of my old Friend, Mr. *John Hilton*, who was Author and first Publisher of most of these Catches.

> Catches *are* Catches *be they better or worse,*
> *And these may prove hopeful if not spoil'd at Nurse*
> *It's therefore desir'd if any do halt,*
> *That the Judicious may set right the Fault:*
> *In time by this means, they may walk without Crutches,*
> *And merrily please you for your charge, which not much is.*[16]

By the time Henry Playford brought out the 1707 edition of the volume Purcell's catches occupied nearly half the book, and were clearly among the most admired.

THE
PREFACE.

Though neither the Design of the following Papers, nor the Matter which is contain'd in them, stand in need of any thing previous in their Behalf, yet since Custom has almost made it necessary that something should be said in their Recommendation, the Publisher thinks himself oblig'd to give the Reader some Account of what he submits to his Perusal. The Design therefore, as it is for a General Diversion, *so it is intended for a general* Instruction, *that the Persons who give themselves the Liberty of an Evenings Entertainment with their Friends, may exchange the Expence they shall be at in being Sociable, with the Knowledge they shall acquire from it; and their Understanding will be encreased, and a true Friendship may be establish'd among them. The Matter in respect to the Words, ows its Birth to the best Authors; and in respect to the Music, has the most Consummate Masters for its Composers; nor is there any thing which does Violence to good Manners, or commits a Rape, on good Sense in it, but what forwards the Establishment of good Company, the Promotion of good Music, and the Advancement of good Words, which will neither give Offence to the nicest Judgments, or be ingrateful to the most delicate and distinguishing Ears.*

Thus much he thought was necessary, without any farther Vindication, than the Great Names of the Persons who oblig'd the World with the Words, and those who (if any thing can add to such Finish'd Pieces) have given a Lustre to them by their Musical Composures; as Dr. Blow, *and the late Famous*

Mr. Henry Purcell, *whose Catches have deservedly gain'd an Universal Applause.*[17]

> Purcell's catches are famous for their bawdy texts and characters, among them Joan in 'Young John the Gard'ner'.

'Young John the Gard'ner'

Young John the Gard'ner having lately got
A very rich and fertile garden plot.
Bragging to Joan. Quoth he 'So rich ground
For melons cannot in the world be found.'
'That's a damn'd lie', quoth Joan, 'for I can tell
A place that does your garden far excel.'
'Where's that?' says John. 'In mine arse', quoth Joan, 'for there
is a store of dung and water all the year.'[18]

> In other catches texts apparently innocent became ribald with the overlapping of voices. The authors of the catches, however, did not confine themselves to such themes, and they recorded many of the important political events of the day. The 'Song with Music on the 7 Bishops', the catch 'True Englishmen drink a good health' to an anonymous verse of 1689, celebrated the stand taken by William Sancroft, Archbishop of Canterbury, and six others. They wished to be excused from reading out in their churches James II's Declaration of Indulgence suspending penal laws against Catholics and Nonconformists, and refusal to give sureties for good behaviour resulted in their incarceration in the Tower. Their later trial and acquittal hastened James into exile.

'Song with Music on the 7 Bishops'

True Englishmen drink a good health to the miter:
Let our Church forever flourish, tho' her enemies spight her;
May their cunning and forces no longer prevail,
But their malice, as well as their arguments, fail;
Then remember the Sev'n, who supported our cause,
As stout as our martyrs, and as just as our laws.[19]

Most catches, of course, were simply entertaining, and played
on a variety of linguistic tricks, as shown in the following
rebus on Henry Purcell's name. Originally written in Latin
by Mr Tomlinson, it was set as a catch by Mr Lenton, and
included in the second book of *The Pleasant Musical Companion* (1701).

A Rebus on Mr. *Hen Purcell's* Name

The Mate to a Cock, and Corn tall as wheat
Is his Christian name, who in music's compleat;
His surname begins with the grace of a cat,
And concludes with the house of a hermit, note that;
His skill and performance each auditor wins,
But the poet deserves a good kick on the shins.[20]

In 'A Song in Commendation of the Viol' the performers
were required to imitate sounds spelt out in the text.

'A Song in Commendation of the Viol'

Of all the instruments that are
None with the viol, can compare.
Mark how the strings their order keep
With a whet, whet, whet and a sweep, sweep, sweep.
But above all this still abounds
With a zingle, zingle, zingle and a zit, zan, zounds.[21]

The entertainment derived from these pieces must have been
great. In the case of 'A Song in Commendation of the Viol'
we learn from Hawkins:

The reverend Mr. Subdean Gostling played on the viol da gamba, and
loved not the instrument more than Purcell hated it. They were very
intimate, as must be supposed, and lived together upon terms of friendship; nevertheless, to vex Mr. Gostling, Purcell got some one to write
[a] mock eulogium on the viol, which he set in a form of round for three
voices.[22]

The later eighteenth century was unable to cope with Purcell's
apparent failure to restrict himself to serious music of stature.

> Hawkins censoriously refers to his 'mirth and good humour,
> which seem to have been habitual to him', and continues:

this perhaps is the best excuse that can be made for those connexions and
intimacies with Brown and others, which show him not to have been very
nice in the choice of his company. Brown spent his life in taverns and
alehouses; the Hole in the Wall in Baldwin's Gardens was the citadel in
which he baffled the assaults of creditors and bailiffs, at the same time
that he attracted thither such as thought his wit atoned for his profligacy.
Purcell seems to have been of that number, and to merit censure for
having prostituted his invention, by adapting music to some of the most
wretched ribaldry that was ever obtruded on the world for humour. The
house of Owen Swan, a vintner in Bartholemew-lane, humorously called
Cobweb-hall, was also a place of great resort for the musical wits of that
day; as also a house in Wych-street, behind the New Church in the
Strand, within time of memory known by a sign of Purcell's head, a half
length; the dress a brown full-bottomed wig, and a green night-gown,
very finely executed. The name of the person who last kept it as a tavern
was Kennedy, a good performer on the bassoon, and formerly in the
opera band.[23]

> Early editors of the catches and glees deleted the words and
> texts of which Hawkins so strongly disapproved, and the
> Purcell Society's collected works contain some fascinating new
> and altered texts calculated to soothe the sensibilities of their
> subscribers. The catch 'Tom the Taylor', not clearly attributed
> to Purcell, but probably from his hand, is a case in point.
> The unbowdlerized text is as follows:

'Tom the Taylor'

Tom, making a mantua for a lass of pleasure
Pull'd out his long and lawful measure
But quickly found, tho' woundily streight lac'd, Sir,
Nine inches wou'd not half surround her waist, Sir.
Three inches more at length brisk Tom advances,
Yet all too short to reach her swinging haunches.[24]

For the edition published in 1922 W. Barclay Squire
provided a cleaned-up version.

'Tom the Taylor'

Tom making a manteau for a lady's pleasure,
It was too small and wrong in measure,
He quickly found, tho' woundily tight-laced, sir,
Nine inches would not half surround her waist, sir;
Three inches more he adds, to make it bigger,
Yet all too small to span her buxom figure.[25]

The alterations to this text – and, indeed, to some others –
do not remove all the innuendo, and it seems likely that the
readings of the catches were not entirely accurate. Such an
attitude is perhaps to be expected in nineteenth-century
England, but it is surprising that it is still to be found today.
In the version of 'My lady's coachman, John' published by
the Oxford University Press in 1987 the word 'cunt' is
replaced with a dash an act which, considering the sentiments
of some of the catches, seems pointless prudery.

The plight of the Seven Bishops is a reminder that England
was a country politically troubled, and interwoven with these
troubles were the difficulties facing those of any denomination
other than Anglican. In the period immediately after Purcell
left the Chapel Royal clear demonstration of the Anglican
faith was essential. By the early 1680s his religious observance
cannot have been above suspicion, for he was forced to take
communion in public in 1683. Although the precise reason
for this remains unknown, Westrup has posited that it was
the result of the enforcement of the laws against dissenters in
the wake of recent political unrest. Whatever the reason, the
authorities were concerned enough to have the document
sworn in court on 4 February 1683.

Bartholemew Wormell, minister of the parish and pari[sh] church of
Margaret's, Westminster, and Giles Burrowde[ll] churchwarden of the
same parish and parish church [do] hereby certify that Mr. Henry
Pursal, one of His Majesty's Chapel, upon the Lord's Day commonly
Sunday, being the fourth day of February instant [imme]diately after
divine service and sermon, did in the parish church aforesaid receive the
sacrament of the Lord's Supper according to the usage of the Church of

England. In witness hereof we the said minister and churchwarden have set our hands the fourth day of February 1682/3.

> Bartho. Wormell, Minister
> Giles Borrowdell, Churchwarden

We Moses Snow and Robert Tanner of Westminster do severally make oath that they do know the said Hen. Pursal now present here in court, and doth deliver the certificate above written and do further severally make oath that they did see the said Henry Pursal receive the sacrament of the Lord's Supper at the time and place, and in the manner above certified, and that they did also see the certificate above written, subscribed by the above-named minister and church warden.

Iur in Cur apud Westm.   Moses Snow
die Lure & vi di Apr.   Robert Tanner
Anno Regni Regis Cordi Scdi.

4. ii. 1682/3[26]

III

The *Sonnata's of III Parts* and
a battle for an organ

In 1683 Purcell published his *Sonnata's of III Parts*, a major volume containing twelve works. The composer himself made claims for their 'Italian' style, something as difficult to quantify then as it is today, though everyone at the time seemed to be clear about what they meant.

ROGER NORTH
(1653–1734)

The English lawyer, polymath and musician Roger North produced some of the most vigorous, bitchy and astute but often prejudiced music criticism ever written. His direct commentary on Purcell is, sadly, limited, for Purcell is generally discussed in the context of broader issues of performance. Further, he had a penchant for Italian music which gives his writing an unhelpful bias.

Then rose up the Noble Purcell, the Jenkins of his time, or more. He was a match for all sorts of designes in musick. Nothing came amiss to him. He imitated the Itallian sonnata and (bating a litle too much of the labour) outdid them. And raising up operas and musick in the theaters, to a credit, even of fame as farr as Italy, where *Sig*ʳ *Purcell* was courted no less than at home . . .

And the master's here began to imitate them [the Italians], wittness Mʳ H. Purcell in his noble set of sonnatas, which however clog'd with somewhat of an English vein, for which they are unworthily despised, are very artificiall and good musick.[1]

'Clog'd with somewhat of an English vein' they undoubtedly were in comparison with the more frivolous Italian style of the early eighteenth century. But had North been writing in the 1680s, his view might have been different. Indeed, when he was commenting on Purcell's operatic music of the 1690s,

his opinion of the composer's efforts at the Italian style had
undergone a marked change.

Then followed the *Circe* and *King Arthur* by the Orfeus Brittanicus M^r H.
Purcell, who unhappily began to shew his great skill before the reforme
of musick *al'Italliana*, and while he was warm in the persuit of it, dyed.[2]

> North makes no distinction between what are clearly two
> different Italian styles – a style distinguishable in English
> music in the Restoration and another, later, Corellian mode
> – and gives an interesting but erroneous account of 'its' intro-
> duction into England.

There was 2 circumstances which concurred to convert the English
Musick intirely over from the French to the Italian taste. One was the
coming over of old Nicholai Matteis; he was a sort of precursor who
made way for what was to follow. He had bin in England divers years
before these enterteinements came forewards, and lived in the citty where
he found some *patroni* that incouraged him . . .

His profession was the violin and guittar, but withall an accomplisht
musitian, and I know no master fitt to be named with Corelli but him; all
his compositions are full of the most artfull harmony, and his fire
exquisite . . . The other circumstance I hinted, was the numerous traine of
yong travellers of the best quallity and estates, that about this time went over
to Itally and resided at Rome and Venice, where they heard the best musick
and learnt of the best masters; and as they went out with a favour derived
from old Nichola, they came home confirmed in the love of the Itallian
manner, and some contracted no litle skill and proved exquisite performers.

Then came over Correlly's first consort that cleared the ground of all
other sorts of musick whatsoever. By degrees the rest of his consorts, and at
last the conciertos came, all which are to musitians like the bread of life.[3]

> Purcell must have come up against the Italian style very early
> on. When he called on Lord Sandwich in 1663, Pepys found
> Captain Cooke and his boys rehearsing an anthem for the
> Chapel Royal.

And after that was done, Captain Cooke and his two boys did sing some
Italian songs, which I must in a word say I think was fully the best
Musique that I ever yet heard in all my life – and it was to me a very
great pleasure to hear them.[4]

Pepy's also recounts the following evening with Thomas Killigrew, the manager of the Theatre Royal in Bridges Street.

By and by with my Lord Brouncker by coach to his house, there to hear
some Italian Musique; and here we met Tom Killigrew, Sir Rob. Murray,
and the Italian Seignor Baptista – who hath composed a play in Italian
for the Opera which T. Killigrew doth intend to have up; and here he
did sing one of the acts . . . He [Killigrew] tells me that he hath gone
several times, eight or ten times he tells me, hence to Rome to hear good
music; so much he loves it, though he never did sing or play a note . . .
That he hath gathered nine Italians from several Courts in Christendome
to come to make a consort for the King, which he doth give *200l* a year
apiece to, but badly paid . . . Baptista tells me that Jiacomo Charissimi
is still alive at Rome, who was maister to Vincentio, who is one of the
Italians the King hath here, and the chief composer of them. My great
wonder is how this man doth do to keep in memory so perfectly the music
of that whole Act, both for the voice and for the instrument too . . .
Saturdy next is appointed to meet again at my Lord Brouncker's lodgings
and there to have the whole Quire of Italians . . . and one thing more,
that by hearing this man tonight, and I think Captain Cooke tomorrow
and the Quire of Italians on Saturday, I shall be truly able to distinguish
which of them pleases me truly best.[5]

It was not only style in music but style in performance which
could be considered Italianate, as one anonymous author, cited
by John Playford, shows when commenting on the Italian
manner of singing.

A brief Discourse of the Italian *manner of Singing; wherein is set down the
Use of those Graces in Singing, as the* Trill *and* Gruppo, *used in* Italy, *and
now in* England: *Written some Years since by an* English *Gentleman, who
had lived long in* Italy, *and being returned, Taught the same here.*[6]

The author goes on to claim an education in the Italian style.

Hitherto I have not put forth to the view of the World those Fruits of
my Musick Studies employed about that Noble manner of Singing, which
I learnt of my Master the famous *Scipione del Palla* in *Italy*; nor my
Compositions of *Ayres* Composed by me, which I saw frequently practised
by the most famous Singers in *Italy*, both Men and Women: But seeing
many of them go about maim'd and spoil'd, and that those long winding

Points were ill performed, I therefore devised to avoid that old manner
of running *Division* which has been hitherto used, being indeed more
proper for Wind and Stringed Instruments than for the Voice: And seeing
that there is made now adays an indifferent and confused use of those
excellent Graces and Ornaments to the good and true manner of *Singing*,
which we call *Trills* and *Grupps*, *Exclamations* of *Increasing* and *Abating*
of the Voice, of which I do intend in this my Discourse to leave some
Foot-prints, that others may attain to this excellent manner of Singing.[7]

> After discussing the application of Italian-style ornaments, he
> gives advice on how to produce the trill which he has been
> discussing.

*Our Author having briefly set forth this chief or most usual Grace in Singing,
called the* Trill, *which, as he saith very right, is by a beating in the Throat
on the Vowel* (ah); *some observe that it is rather the shaking of the* Uvula *or
Pallate on the Throat, in one sound upon a Note: For the attaining of this,
the most sure and ready way is by imitation of those who are perfect in the
same; yet I have heard of some that have attained it after this manner, in the
singing a plain Song, of 6 Notes up and 6 down, they have in the midst of every
Note beat or shaked with their finger upon their Throat, which by often
practice came to do the same Notes exactly without.*[8]

> To this note the editor appends a description of a music
> practice which he appears to have attended.

*It was also my chance to be in company with some Gentlemen at a Musical
Practice, which sung their Parts very well, and used this Grace (called the*
Trill*) very exactly: I desired to know their Tutor, they told me I was their
Tutor, for they never had any other but this my* **Introduction** : *That (I
answered) could direct them but in the Theory, they must needs have a better help
in the Practick, especially in attaining to sing the* Trill *so well. One of them
made this Reply (which made me smile) I used, said he, at my first learning the*
Trill, *to imitate that breaking of a Sound in the Throat which Men use when
they Lewer their Hawks, as* he-he-he-he-he; *which he used slow at first, and
after more swift on several Notes, higher and lower in sound, 'till he became
perfect therein.*[9]

> The debate between those advocating English music and those
> supporting music in the Italian style continued well into the

eighteenth century. Purcell's music played a role in many of
these discussions, including John Macky's.

THE *English* affect more the *Italian* than the *French* Musick; and their
own Compositions are between the *Gravity* of the first and the *Levity* of
the other. They have had several great Masters of their own. *Henry
Purcell's* works in that Kind are esteemed beyond *Lully's* everywhere;
and they have now a good many very Eminent Masters; but the Taste
of the Town being at this Day all *Italian*, it is a great discouragement
to them.[10]

> The printing of Purcell's sonatas 'in the Italian way' which
> eventually appeared in 1683 gives an interesting sidelight on
> publishing during this period. Purcell published his proposals
> for the volume and gentlemen inspected those proposals at
> Mr William Hall's house or the shops of John Carr and John
> Playford; if they liked what they saw, they subscribed to the
> volume. When the printing was finished, Purcell offered a
> final chance to those who had missed out.

These are to give Notice to all Gentlemen that have subscribed to the
Proposals Published by Mr. Henry Purcel for the Printing [of] his
Sonata's of three Parts for two Violins and Base to the Harpsecord or
Organ, That the said Books are now compleatly finished, and shall be
delivered to them upon the 11th of June next: And if any who have not
yet Subscribed, shall before that time Subscribe, according to the said
Proposals, (which is Ten Shillings the whole sett) which are at Mr.
William Hall's house in Norfolk-street, or at Mr. Playford's and Mr
Carr's Shops in the Temple; for the said Books will not after that time
be Sold under 15s. the Sett.[11]

> This was in May. By June those with valid subscription notes
> were being asked to call at Purcell's house and collect their
> goods.

Whereas the time is now expired, this is therefore to desire those Persons
that have subscribed to Mr Henry Purcel's Sonata's, to repair to his house
in St Anns' Lane beyond Westminster-Abby, or to send Proposal-Paper
they received with the Receipt to it when they Subscribed, and those who
subscribed without a Paper or Receipt, to bring a Note under the Persons

Hand to whom they Subscribed, that there may be no mistake, and they shall receive their Books, paying the remaining part of the Money.[12]

> By November Purcell's obligations to the subscribers had been discharged, and the volume was made available to the general public.

These are to give Notice to all Lovers of Musick concerning the New Musical Compositions, called SONATA's, lately Published by Mr. Henry Purcell, that (the Subscribers being satisfied) they are now to be Sold at these following places, viz. at Mr. John Playford's, and Mr. John Carrs shops in the Temple, and at Mr. Henry Rogers, Bookseller in Westminster Hall.[13]

> The dedicatee of the collection was King Charles II.

To his Sacred Maj.^ty
May it please yor Maj.^ty
I had not assum'd the confidence of laying y^e following Compositions at your Sacred feet; but that as they are the immediate Results of your Majesties Royall favour, and benignity to me (which have made me what I am) So, I am constrain'd to hope, I may presume, amongst Others of your Majesties over=oblig'd and altogether undeserving Subjects, that your Maj^ty will with your accustom'd Clemency, Vouchsafe to Pardon the best Endeavours of Yo.^r Majesties

> *Most Humble*
> *and most Obedient*
> *Subject and Servant*
>
> *Henry Purcell*[14]

> Purcell's claim for the Italianate character of the sonatas was set forth in the preface.

Ingenuous Reader,
Instead of an elaborate harangue on the beauty and the charms of Musick (which after all the learned Encomions that words can contrive) commends it Self best by the performances of a skilful hand, and an angelical voice: I shall Say but a very few things by way of Preface, concerning the following Book, and its Author: for its Author, he has faithfully endeavour'd a just imitation

of the most fam'd Italian Masters; principally, to bring the Seriousness and gravity of that Sort of Musick into vogue, and reputation among our Country-men, whose humor, 'tis time now, should begin to loath the levity, and balladry of our neighbours: The attempt he confesses to be bold, and daring, there being Pens and Artists of more eminent abilities, much better qualify'd for the imployment than his, or himself, which he well hopes these his weak endevours, will in due time provoke, and enflame to a more acurate undertaking. He is not asham'd to own his unskilfulness in the Italian Language; but that's the unhappiness of his Education, which cannot justly be accounted his fault, however he thinks he may warrantably affirm, that he is not mistaken in the power of the Italian Notes, or elegancy of their Compositions, which he would recommend to the English Artists. There has been neither care, nor industry wanting, as well in contriving, as revising the whole Work; which had been abroad in the world much Sooner, but that he has now thought fit to cause the whole Thorough Bass to be Engraven, which was a thing quite besides his first Resolutions. It remains only that the English Practitioner be enform'd, that he will find a few terms of Art perhaps unusual to him, the chief of which are these following: Adagio *and* Grave, *which import nothing but a very slow movement:* Presto Largo, Poco Largo, *or* Largo *by it Self, a middle movement:* Allegro, *and* Vivace, *a very brisk, Swift, or fast movement:* Piano, *Soft. The Author has no more to add, but his hearty wishes, that his Book may fall into no other hands but theirs who carry Musical Souls about them; for his is willing to flatter himself into a belief, that with Such his labours will Seem neither unpleasant, or unprofitable.* [15]

> The excuse for the delay in the publication of the sonatas mentioned by Purcell has usually been taken at face value, but the fact that it was the first music publication engraved on a copperplate to appear in England is suggestive of further reasons.
> Purcell himself appears to have enjoyed performing the pieces in an ensemble. Francis North, Lord Keeper of the Great Seal to Charles II, spent some of his spare time playing them with the composer, according to Roger North.

After business took up most of his time, and he had litle to spare, this instrument was less courted by him, the rather because his great desire to use the upper part, which was not in time to be learnt, made him less delight in a consort-base part. But yet, even when he had the Great Seal, he caused the devine Purcell to bring his Itallian manner'd compositions; and with him on his harpsicord, my self and another violin, wee performed them more than once, of which Mr Purcell was not a little proud, nor was it a common thing for one of his dignity to be so enterteined.[16]

> Perhaps it was from one of these trio sonata sessions that Roger North remembered a sharp remark of the composer's about the inverse ratio of quality and success.

The noble Purcell lately stole[n] from us into another world . . . used to mark what did not take for the best musick, it being his constant observation that what took least, was really best.[17]

THE 'BATTLE OF THE ORGANS'

> It is Roger North, too, who gives us some account of the great 'Battle of the Organs'. Throughout his life Purcell was called on by various bodies to advise or adjudicate on the building or repair of church organs. One such, its case still extant, was at the Guild Church of St Katherine Cree, Leadenhall Street, where the accounts include payments for Purcell's coach hire.

An account of moneys given, received, and paid for the erecting of an organ and building a gallery in the parish church of St Katherine Cree. £124. £77. £80. £44. received many subscriptions of £11, £10, 5, 6, 2, 1, etc.
Payments.
   Paid Mr. Bernard Smith for making the organ as contract £250.0.0.
   Paid various sums for gallery £65 etc.
   Spent on Mr. Pursell and Mr. Smith 14/-
   Paid coach hire for Dr. Blowe and Mr Pursell 5/-
   For curtains and curtain rings £1. 18. 4*d*.
Altogether, a sum of £355. 11. 3*d*. was paid out.[18]

> Purcell was required to play the organ and give his final approval, and then select an organist in what seems to have been an impressive blind contest.

Doctor Blow, Mr. Purcell, Mr. Mosses, Mr. Fforcell this day appeared at our church, Mr. Purcell was desired to play and did play upon the organ, and after he had done playing they all reported to the vestry that in their judgments the organ was a good organ, and was performed and completed according to contract . . . Mr. Nicolls, Mr. Beach, Mr. Snow, and Mr. Heath this day appearing and according to an order of the last Vestry did severally play upon the organ in the audience of the above Dr. Blow, Mr. Purcell, Mr. Mosse, and Mr. Fforcell, and several parishioners of this parish. And the said Dr. Blow, Mr. Purcell, Mr. Mosse, and Mr. Fforcell after the said Mr. Nicolls, Mr. Beach, Mr. Snow and Mr. Heath had done playing reported to the Vestry that the third person that played (which fell out to be Mr. Snow) did in their judgements play the best and most skillfully of them all, and that the first that played (which fell out to be Mr. Beach) played next best. And thereupon the Vestry proceeded to a choice of an organist, and the said Mr. Niccolls, Mr Beach, Mr. Snow and Mr. Heath being put in nomination for an organist, and every person of the Vestry then present giving this vote by scratch of pen or scrutiny. The choice by majority of hands continued . . . fell upon Mr. Snowe who had eight hands and Mr. Beach but five hands, and Mr. Niccolls and Mr. Heath but one hand apiece. And the said Mr. Snowe being afterwards made acquainted with the said choice, gratefully accepted of the said place.[19]

> More dramatic – and, from this distance, more entertaining – was the earlier 'Battle of the Organs' between the builders Renatus Harris and Father Smith over the commission for the new organ for the Temple Church. As North commented:

And worse happened upon a competition for an organ at the Temple Church in which the 2 competitors, the best artists in Europe, Smith and Harris, were but just not ruined.[20]

> He concluded:

So much a mistake it is to force artists upon competition, for all but one are sure to malccontents.[21]

> A more detailed account of the battle was given by Thomas Tudway, though he is wrong in one particular: G. B. Draghi, not Lully, played Harris's organ.

Upon the decease of Mr. Dallans and the elder Harris, Mr. Renatus Harris and Father Smith became great rivals in their employment, and several tryals of skill there were betwixt them on several ocasions; but the famous contest between these two artists was at the Temple church, where a new organ was going to be erected towards the latter end of K. Charles the second's time: both made friends for that employment; but as the society could not agree about who should be the man, the Master of the Temple and the Benchers proposed they both should set up an organ on each side of the church, which in about half a year or three quarters of a year was done accordingly; Dr. Blow and Mr. Purcell, who was then in his prime, shewed and played Father Smith's organ on appointed days to a numerous audience; and, till the other was heard, everybody believed that Father Smith certainly would carry it.

Mr. Harris brought Mr. Lully, organist to Queen Catherine, a very eminent master, to touch his organ, which brought Mr. Harris's organ into that vogue; they thus continued vying with one another near a twelve-month. Then Mr. Harris challenged Father Smith to make additional stops against a set time; these were the Vox-humane, the Cremona or Violin stop, the double Courtel or bass Flute, with some others I may have forgot.

These stops, as being newly invented, gave great delight and satisfaction to the numerous audience; and were so well imitated on both sides, that it was hard to judge the advantage of either. At last it was left to my Lord Chief Justice Jeffries, who was of that house, and he put an end to the controversy by pitching upon Father Smith's organ; so Mr. Harris's organ was taken away without loss of reputation, and Mr Smith's remains to this day . . .

The Honourable Roger North who was in London at the time of the contention at the Temple Church, says, in his memoirs of music, that the competition between Smith and Harris, the two best artists in Europe, was carried on with such violence by the friends of both sides that they 'were just not ruined'. Indeed, old Roseingrave assured me that the partizans for each candidate in the fury of their zeal proceeded to the most mischievous and unwarrantable acts of hostility; and that in the night preceding the last trial of the reed stops, the friends of Harris cut the bellows of Smith's organ in such a manner that when the time came for playing upon it no wind could be conveyed into the wind-chest. [22]

IV

Two coronations and a revolution

JOHN EVELYN
(1620–1706)

The death of Charles II on 2 February 1685 was recorded by the God-fearing diarist John Evelyn. After Balliol College, Oxford, he entered the Middle Temple in 1640, spent some of the Commonwealth years on the Continent and became active in court affairs at the Restoration. His public appointments included his post as one of the commissioners of the Privy Seal and the treasurership of Greenwich Hospital, and he was a member of the Royal Society. Evelyn was a less astute observer than Pepys and his diary (found in a laundry basket in 1817) was not kept as a journal; bits of history drawn from published sources were clearly added retrospectively. Evelyn does not record a meeting with Purcell and only once mentions his music, but his connections with the court gave him ample opportunity for observation.

[I am never to forget the unexpressable luxury, & prophanesse, gaming, & all dissolution, and as it were total forgetfullnesse of God (it being Sunday Evening) which this day sennight, I was witnesse of; the King, sitting & toying with his Concubines Portsmouth, Cleaveland, & Mazarine: &c: A french boy singing love songs, in that glorious Gallery, whilst about 20 of the greate Courtiers & other dissolute persons were at Basset round a large table, a bank of at least 2000 in Gold before them, upon which two Gent: that were with me made reflexions with astonishment, it being a sceane of uttmost vanity; and surely as they thought would never have an End: six days after was all in the dust.][1]

> Charles, buried (as Evelyn said) 'very obscurely', was succeeded by his brother, James, who had openly confessed his Catholicism and married the Catholic Mary, sister of the Duke of Modena, in 1673. James lost no time in allowing more freedom in worship, and, as Evelyn noted, those of the Catholic faith publicly demonstrated their allegiance.

To my griefe I saw the new pulpet set up in the popish oratory at W—hall, for the Lent preaching, Masse being publiqly saied, & the Romanists swarming at Court with greater confidence than had ever ben seene in England since the Reformation, so as every body grew Jealous to what

this would tend; A Parliament was now also summond, and greate industry
used to obtaine Elections which might promote the Court Interest: Most
of the Corporations being now by their new Charters in power to make
what returnes of members they pleased: Most of the Judges likewise
having given their opinions that his Majestie might still take the
Costomes, which to foure Judges (<esteem'd> the best Lawyers) seemed
against the Act of Parliament which determines it with the Kings life.[2]

> Catholicism may have played a part in Evelyn's lack of interest
> in the coronation.

Was the day of his Majesties Coronation, the Queene was also crown'd,
the solemnity very magnificent, as the particulars are set forth in print:
The Bish: of Ely preached, but (to the greate sorrow of the people) no
Sacrament, as ought to have ben: However the King beginns his reigne
with greate expectations and hopes of much reformation as to the former
vices, & prophanesse both of Court & Country:

   Having ben present at our late Kings Coronation, I was not ambitious
of seing this Ceremonie.[3]

FRANCIS SANDFORD
(1630–94)

> Among those who 'set forth in print' the details of the coron-
> ation was Francis Sandford, Lancaster Herald at Arms. His
> lavishly illustrated volume describes the elaborate preparations
> under way from February, and by the beginning of April
> Sandford was able to record the provision of the dress for the
> musicians at the ceremony.

And it was Further Order'd the same Day, That the *Lord Treasurer* give
Directions for Two *Faldstools* with Coverings and Cushions for Her
Majesty, and for the providing of *Habits* for the 36 MUSICIANS who
were to attend His *Majesties Coronation:* Both which Particulars his *Lordship* by Letters of the 13 and 14 of *April* directed the *Commissioners* of
the *Great-Wardrobe* to provide which they accordingly did; and on the 16
of *April* there was delivered to Dr. *Nicholas Staggins*, as One of His
Majesties Composers, Five Yards of Fine *Scarlet Cloth* for a *Mantle*, and
to each of the 35 *Musitians* here-after named, Four Yards.[4]

Purcell was one of the musicians who received the cloth; he walked among the basses in 'The *GRAND PROCEEDING* to Their *MAJESTIES* CORONATION, from WESTMIN-STER-HALL to the Collegiate-Church of St. *PETER* in WESTMINSTER.

GENTLEMEN of His *Majesties* CHAPEL-ROYAL, in *Surplices*, with *Mantles* over them, Four a-Breast, *viz.*

Counter-Tenors.

1. Mr. *Michael Wise*, supplied by *Edw. Morton*.

2. Mr. *Tho. Heywood*, supplied by Dr. *Uvedal*.

3. Mr. *John Abel*, supplied by *Aug. Benford*.

4. Mr. *Josias Boucher*.

5. Mr. *William Turner*.

6. Mr. *Thomas Richardson*.

7. Mr. *John Goodgroom*.

8. Mr. *Nathaniel Watkins*.

Tenors.

9. Mr. *Morgan Harris*.

10. Mr. *Alphonso Marsh*.

11. Mr. *Henry Frost*.

12. *William Powel* Clerk.

13. Mr. *James Cobb*.

14. Mr. *Edward Bardock*.

15. *Henry Smith* Cl. supplied by *Geo. Hart*.

16. *John Sayer* Clerk.

Basses.

17. *Richard Hart*.

18. *Samuel Bentham* Clerk.

19. *Leon. Woodson* Clerk.

20. *John Gostlin* Clerk.

21. *Henry Purcel* Organist of *Westminster*.

22. *Nathaniel Vestment*.

23. *John Charole* Clerk.

24. *Andrew Tebeck* Clerk.

25. *George Bettenham*.

26. *James Hart* Clerk.

27. *Blaze White* Clerk.

28. *George Yardley* Clerk.

29. *Tho. Blagrave* Clerk of the Check to the Gentlemen of the Chapel.	30. *Nich. Staggins* Dr. in Musick, and Master of the Kings Musick.	31. *Joh. Blow* Dr. in Mus. M^r of the *Childr.* of the *Chapel & Organist*, suppl. by *Fra. Forcer.*	32. *William Child* Dr. in Musick, Eldest Gentleman of the Chapel.[5]

> While preparations were in train, Purcell was engaged in the
> erection of a second organ, to be used for the ceremony and
> then dismantled.

To Henry Purcell, for so much money by him disbursed and craved for
providing and setting up an Organ in the Abbey Church of Westminster
for the solemnity of the Coronation, and for the removing of the same,
and other services performed in His said Majesty's Chapel since 25th of
March 1685 according to a bill signed by the Bishop of London . . .

£34.12[6]

> The congregation heard nine anthems in all. The first was
> Purcell's *I was glad when they said unto me.*

By this time the KING and QUEEN being entred the Church, were
received by the *Dean* and *Prebendaries*, who, with the *Choir* of *Westminster*,
proceeding little before Their MAJESTIES, Sung the full *Anthem.*[7]

> Anthems by John Blow, Henry Lawes, William Turner and
> William Child were sung during the service. Then:

The QUEEN being thus ANOINTED and CROWNED, and having
received all *Her Royal ornaments*, the *Choirs* sang the following *Verse-
Anthem*, performed by the whole *Consort* of *Voices* and *Instruments*.[8]

> Purcell's anthem *My heart is inditing* followed. Purcell was
> clearly occupied as the King and Queen prepared to process
> out of the Abbey, for 'the *Organs* [were] playing all the
> while'. The congregation, though not, apparently, the
> musicians, moved to Westminster Hall for the coronation
> feast.

Whilst the KING and QUEEN were in St. *Edwards Chapel*, the *Officers*
of *Arms* called in *Order* such only as were to return to *Westminster-Hall*:
(for the *Prebendaries* of *Westminster* and the *Choirs* were not to go back in

the *Proceeding* to the *Hall*,) and drew them down, out of the *Choir*, into
the Body of the *Church*.⁹

As Sandford put it:

All the Way, from the *Church* to the *Hall*, the *Drums* beat, the *Trumpets*
sounded, and the Vast Multitude of Beholders, filling the air with Loud
Acclamations and Shouts, and hearty prayers for Their MAJESTIES
Long Life and *Prosperity*, expressed not only the most Ardent and Dutiful
Affections, but also the utmost height of Joy and Satisfaction.¹⁰

> It comes as no surprise, after the erratic payments made to
> musicians under Charles II, to find that the Stuart tradition
> continued under James: in November payments were just
> being made to Nicholas Staggins for copying music and sup-
> plying outside instrumentalists required for the coronation
> ceremony.

These are to pray and require you to pay or cause to be paid unto Dr.
Nicholas Staggins, Master of his Maᵗˢ Musick, the sume of £19. 11s.
6d. for faire writeing of a composition for His Majesty's coronation day
from the originall score the 6 parts, for drawing ye said composition into
forty severall parts for trumpetts, hautboyes, violins, tennors, basses,
pricker's dyett included, for ruled paper, penns ink, and chamber rent,
and disburst in providing severall musitians for ye coronation day who
were not His Majesty's servants.¹¹

> James's reign was to prove an unhappy one. He was badly
> advised and politically indiscreet, and his religion, a matter
> of concern before he ascended the throne, became more and
> more problematic. John Evelyn made no attempt to conceal
> his thoughts:

I was to heare the Musique of the Italians in the new Chapel, now first
of all opned at White-hall publiquely for the Popish Service: Nothing
can be finer than the magnificent Marble work & Architecture at the
End, where are 4 statues representing st. Joh: st. Petre, st. Paule, & the
Church, statues in white marble, the worke of Mr. Gibbons, with all the
carving & Pillars of exquisite art & greate cost: . . . The Thrones where
the K. & Q: sits is very glorious in a Closset above just opposite to the
Altar: Here we saw the Bishop in his Miter, & rich Copes, with 6 or 7:

Jesuits & others in Rich Copes richly habited, often taking off, & putting on the Bishops Miter, who sate in a Chaire with Armes pontificaly, was adored, & censed by 3 Jesuits in their Copes, then he went to the Altar & made divers Cringes there, censing the Images, & glorious Tabernacle placed upon the Altar, & now & then changing place; The Crosier (which was of silver) put into his hand, with a world of mysterious Ceremony the Musique pla<y>ing & singing: & so I came away: not believing I should ever have lived to see such things in the K. of Englands palace, after it had pleas'd God to inlighten this nation; but our greate sinn, has (for the present) Eclips'd the Blessing, which I hope he will in mercy & his good time restore to its purity.[12]

> Evelyn's anti-Catholic stance did not stop him attending services at court.

I heard the famous *Cifeccio* (Eunuch) sing, in the new popish chapell this afternoone, which was indeede very rare, & with greate skill: He came over from Rome, esteemed one of the best voices in *Italy*, much crowding, little devotion.[13]

> Evelyn heard Siface again in company with Samuel Pepys.

I heard the famous Singer the Eunuch *Cifacca*, esteemed the best in *Europe* & indeede his holding out & delicatenesse in extending & loosing a note with that incomparable softnesse, and sweetenesse was admirable: For the rest, I found him a meere wanton, effeminate child; very Coy, & prowdly conceited to my apprehension: He touch'd the Harpsichord to his Voice rarely well, & this was before a select number of some particular persons whom Mr. Pepys (Secretary of the Admiralty & a greate lover of Musick) invited to his house, where the meeting was, & this obtained by peculiar favour & much difficulty of the Singer, who much disdained to shew his talent to any but Princes.[14]

> 'Siface' was the nickname acquired by the Italian singer Giovanni Francesco Grossi for his performance in Cavalli's *Scipione africano* in 1671. By 1679 he had entered the service of the Duke of Modena, and in 1687 was sent to England to entertain Queen Mary, the Duke's sister. As Evelyn suggests, he was temperamental; Purcell, probably ironically, composed a short harpsichord piece entitled *Sefauchi's Farewell* towards the end of the year.

James's indiscretions – the already mentioned affair of the
Seven Bishops, his appointment of Catholics to ecclesiastical
posts, his attitude to parliament and his violation of the rights
of the universities of Oxford and Cambridge – were now
threatening the stability of the country. Evelyn described how
the population finally rebelled. His account is interesting not
for its accuracy – indeed, it is flawed – but for its evident
confusion. Such is the way news must have reached Purcell.

[The rabble people demolish all Papists Chapells & severall popish Lords
& Gent: house<s>, especialy that of the Spanish Ambassador, which
they pillaged & burnt his Library &c:] . . .

. . . The King flies to sea, [putts in at Feversham for ballast is rudely
detained by the people: comes back to W<hite>hall.]

The Pr: of Orange now advanc'd to Windsor, is invited by the King
to St. James, the messenger sent was the E. of Feversham the general of
the forces: who going without Trumpet or passeport is detained prisoner
by the Prince: The Prince accepts the Invitation, but requires his Majestie
to retire to some distant place, that his owne Guards may be quartered
about the palace & Citty: This is taken heinously, so the King gos away
privately to Rochester: Is perswaded to come back: comes on the Sunday;
Goes to masse & dines in publique, a Jesuite says grace: [I was present]
That night a Council, his Majestie refuses to assent to all proposals; gos
away againe to Rochester.[15]

The end came quickly.

The Pr: comes to St. James, fills W-hall (the King taking barge to
Gravesend at 12 a Clock) with Dut<c>h Guard: A Council of Peres
meete about an Expedient to call a parliament: Adjourne to the House of
Lords: The Chancelor, E. of Peterbor, & divers Priests & other taken:
E: of Sunderland flies & divers others, Sir E: Hales, Walker & other
taken & secured: All the world go to see the Prince at St. Jamess where
is a greate Court, there I saw him & severall of my Acquaintance that
come over with him: He is very stately, serious, & reserved: The Eng:
souldiers &c. sent out of Towne to distant quarters: not well pleased:
Divers reports & opinions, what all this will end in; Ambition & faction
feared.[16]

The presence of William of Orange, grandson of Charles I

and James's son-in-law, had been solicited by seven leading
politicians and he was hailed by the country as a deliverer.
His invasion of the kingdom was undertaken in the name of
his wife; they were jointly declared king and queen in February 1689 and their coronation took place on Thursday, 11
April. The *London Gazette* reported that

*the Procession began in this manner. Drums and Trumpets; Six Clerks in
Chancery, two a-Breast (as all the rest of the Proceeding went, Chaplains
having Dignities; Aldermen of* London; *Masters in Chancery; Sollicitor, and
Attorney General; Gentlemen of the Privy Chamber; Judges.*

   Children of Westminster, *and of the King's Chapel; Choir of* Westminster;
and Gentlemen of the Chapel; Prebends of Westminster; *Masters of the Jewel-
house; Privy Councellors not Peers.* [17]

> The rest of the procession followed. Evelyn was more
> interested in events than he had been in 1685, but his descrip-
> tion suggests that there was less grandeur than there had been
> in the past.

I saw the procession both to, & from the Abby church of Westminster,
with the greate feast in Westminster Hall &c: at the Coronation of the
new K William & Q. Mary: That which was different from former
Coronations, was, something altered in the Coronation Oath, concerning
maintaining the Prot: Religion: &c: Dr. Burnet (now made L.B. of
Sarum) preached on with infinite applause: The parliament men had
Scaffolds & places which tooke up one whole side of the Hall: & when
the K & Q. had din'd. The Ceremonie of the Champion, & other services
upon Tenures: The Parliament men were also feasted in the Exchequer
Chamber: . . . Much of the splendor of the proceeding was abated, by
the absence of divers who should have made it up: There being but as
yet 5 Bish: 4. Judges, (no more at present, it seemes [as yet] sworn) &
severall noblemen & greate Ladys wanting: But indeede the Feast was
magnificent: The next day, went the H of Commons & kissed their new
Majesties hands in the Banqueting house. [18]

> The coronation saw Purcell attending to his usual duties,
> including the provision of the second organ. There was,
> though, what is thought to have been a misunderstanding
> about the fees the organist could charge for allowing members
> of the public into the organ gallery, as Hawkins explains.

In the beginning of the year 1689 *he became engaged in a dispute with Dr. Sprat, the then Dean, and the Chapter of Westminster, the occasion whereof was this. It seems that at the coronation of King William and queen Mary, he had received and claimed as his right, the money taken for admission into the organ loft of persons desirous of being near spectators of that ceremony, which for the following reasons must be supposed to have amounted to a considerable sum; the profit arising to the owner of one of the houses at the west end of the Abbey, where only the procession could be viewed, amounted at the last coronation to five hundred pounds. The organ in Purcell's time was on the north side of the choir, and was much nearer to the Altar than now, so that spectators from thence might behold the whole of that august ceremony.*

A sum like that which this must be presumed to have been was worth contending for, and if Purcell had the authority of precedent for his support, he was right in retaining it as a perquisite arising from his office; but his masters thought otherwise, and insisted on it as their due, for in an old chapter book I find the following entry: '18 *April,* 1689, *Mr. Purcell, the organ blower, to pay to Mr. Needham such money as was received by him for places in the organ loft, and in default thereof his place to be declared null and void, and that his stipend or salary be detained in the Treasurer's hands until further orders.' Upon which it may be observed that the penning of it is evidence of great ignorance or malice, in that it describes him by the appellation of blower who was organist of their own church, and in truth the most excellent musician of his time.*[19]

Purcell clearly chose to pay the money and keep his job.

V

Publishing, pedagogy and a passing

HENRY PLAYFORD
(*c.* 1657–1707)

The music publisher and bookseller Henry Playford was the younger son of John Playford (1623–86), the publisher of the volume in which 'Sweet Tyranness' appeared in 1667 and of the *Sonnata's of III Parts* in 1683. If Henry Playford's prefaces showed less missionary zeal than his father's, he was at least innovative, and had a sure instinct for the requirements of the public. In 1688 he produced the first volume of Purcell's *Harmonia Sacra*, though since John Playford died as late as December 1686, this may well have been his father's brainchild. Purcell has twelve pieces in the collection (plus one doubtful and one spurious attribution), and seems to have acted as general editor. The dedicatee was the Bishop of Bath and Wells.

TO THE

RIGHT REVEREND

FATHER in GOD

THOMAS

Lord Bishop of Bath and Wells

This Collection of *Divine Musick* is (with just Veneration) most humbly Dedicated by

His Lordship's
Devoted Servant,
HENRY PLAYFORD.[1]

Playford went on to provide a considerable address to the user of the volume, in which Purcell's role as editor is made plain. (The passages in square brackets were omitted in the second edition.)

TO THE
READER

[THE Approbation which has been given by those of the greatest Skill in *Musick*, and the Encouragement I have met with from a number of worthy Subscribers do give me just reason to hope, that this Collection of *Divine Songs* (tho' the first of this nature extant) will find a kind Reception with the best of Men.]

The Youthful and Gay have already been entertain'd with variety of rare Compositions, where the lighter Sportings of Wit have been Tun'd by the most artful Hands, and made at once to gratify a delicate Ear, and a wanton Curiosity.

I now therefore address to others, who are no less *Musical*, though they are more *Devout*. There are many Pious Persons, who are not only just Admirers, but excellent Judges too, both of *Musick* and *Wit*; to these a singular Regard is due, and their exquisite Relish of the former ought not to be pall'd by an unagreeable Composition of the latter. Divine *Hymns* are therefore the most proper Entertainment for them, which, as they make the sweetest, and indeed the only, Melody to a *Religious Ear*, so are they in themselves the very Glory and Perfection of *Musick*.

For 'tis the meanest and most Mechanical Office of this *Noble Science* to play upon the Ear, and strike the Fancy with a superficial Delight; but when Holy and Spiritual Things are its Subject, it proves of a more subtile and refined Nature, whilst darting it self through the Organs of Sense, it warms and actuates all the Powers of the Soul, and fills the Mind with the brightest and most ravishing Contemplations. *Musick* and *Poetry* have in all Ages been accounted Divine, and therefore they cannot be more naturally employed, than when they are conversant about *Heaven*, that Region of *Harmony*, from whence they are derived.

Now as to this present Collection, I need say no more than that the *Words* were penn'd by such Persons, as are, and have been, very Eminent both for Learning and Piety; and indeed, he that reads them as he ought, will soon find his Affections warm'd, as with a Coal from the Altar, and feel the Breathings of Divine Love from every Line. [As for the *Musical Part*, it was Compos'd by the most Skilful Masters of this Age; and though some of them are now dead, yet their Composures have been review'd by Mr. *Henry Purcell*, whose tender Regard for the Reputation of those great Men, made him careful that nothing should be published, which, through the negligence of Transcribers, might reflect upon their memory.] Here therefore the *Musical* and *Devout* cannot want Matter both to exersize their Skill, and heighten their devotion; to which excellent Purposes that this Book may be truly effectual is the hearty desire of

Your humble Servant,
Henry Playford.[2]

When Playford published the second edition in 1703, Purcell
(now dead) was given short shrift, as the omitted passages
show, and the Bishop of Bath and Wells was replaced by the
Queen as the dedicatee.

To the QUEEN'S
Most
Excellent Majesty:

MADAM,

*THE Best of Authors have been always Presents for the Best of Princes, and
it would have been a great breach of Duty in me, to lay these Excellent
Performances any where but at Your Majesty's Sacred Feet. Your Majesty
has a double Right to their Patronage, from Your Love of Musick, and
affection to Devotion, and as You are an Encourager of Both, so both apply
themselves with all Humility for Your Protection.*

*Your Majesty was pleased to give Mr. Purcell Your Royal Approbation
when Living, and it is Humbly hop'd the Memory of him will not be unpleasing
to You now He is Dead; and though the Publisher has no Merit in himself to
Recommend Him to Your Majesty's Presence, Your Majesty will Graciously
receive what begs Your Acceptance, for the sake of those Ingenious Gentlemen
that Oblig'd the World with these Compositions.*

*The Encouragement of Arts and Sciences is one of the Prerogatives of
Royalty, and the most Glorious Reigns have allways had the Reputation of
being the most Learned. What may we not then expect under Your Majesty's
auspicious Government? This makes me presume to hope, that the Piety of
Words, and Artfulness of the Musick will not appear undeserving of Your
Majesty's Favour. Which if they may be so Happy as to obtain I shall think
it my Glory to continue my great cost and Pains in contributing to the Publick
satisfaction, and ever make it my endeavour to approve my self, Madam,*

You Majesty's most Dutyful,
Most Devoted, and most
Faithful Subject
HENRY PLAYFORD.[3]

The arrival of the second book (in which Purcell had five
pieces, as well as one spurious and two doubtful attributions)
was, like many other musical events, announced in the *Gentleman's Journal.*

A music book intituled *Harmonia Sacra* will shortly be printed, for Mr Playford. I need not say anything more to recommend it to you than that you will find in it many of Mr Henry Purcell's admirable compositions. As they charm all men, they are universally extoll'd, and ev'n those who know him no otherwise than by his notes, are fond of expressing their sense of his merit.[4]

> Playford's dedicated this volume to the multi-talented music collector Henry Aldrich, Dean of Christ Church, Oxford. After his election as a student in 1662 his career followed a pattern of academic appointments, and he was Vice-Chancellor of Oxford from 1692 until 1695. He was also a composer and arranger, and collected a wide variety of Italian music by such composers as Monteverdi and Carissimi – an interesting and appropriate dedicatee for the second book of *Harmonia Sacra*.

To the Reverend
HENRY ALDRICH, D.D.
Dean of *Christ-Church*, and Vice-Chancellor of the
University of *OXFORD*

SIR,
THIS is the Greatest Thing I can do, for the Excellent Musick, Poetry *and* Piety *of these Papers; it has been my Care indeed to save them from Oblivion, but they are Indebted to me now much more, for the Defence and Ornament of Your Name.*

In Addresses of this kind, Men are usually so far from suiting the subject of their Treatises to the Qualifications of the Persons they Apply to, that we may shortly expect to see Musick *Dedicated to the Deaf, as well as* Poetry *to* Aldermen, *and* Prayer-books *to Aetheists; and though generally it is a difficult matter to find a* Worthy Patron *for any One of these Excellencies, yet we happily find them all lodg'd in your self. It has indeed been very seldom known since the Royal Prophet's Time, that any Single Man has been thus Qualified, but they All meet so Eminently in You, (not to mention those other Great Advantages which distinguish You from the rest of the World,) that it had been possible for me to have been at a Loss to whom I should have Addressed my self, Thousands would have named You in the same Instant.*

To make this Collection *Compleat and that it might consist of some of the best Foreign Hands as well as our own, I have at the End inserted some of*

Gratiano's *and* Carissime's *Compositions which you, with the rest of the just Judges of* Musick, *so much Esteem.*

   Pardon me then, Sir, if I presume to beg Your Protection for these Papers, 'tis the utmost of my Fidelity and Love to my Charge; and I shall now have the Glory of Providing better for other Men's Works, than ever the Fondest Author could do for his Own. I am,

SIR,

Your most humble Servant,
Henry. Playford.[5]

   The volume contains some poems on the collections. The one
   by an anonymous poet is addressed to Henry Playford, Henry
   Sacheverell's to both John Blow and Purcell, and Thomas
   Brown's to Purcell alone.

To his unknown Friend, Mr. Henry Purcell, *upon his Excellent Compositions in the First and Second Books of* HARMONIA SACRA.

   Long and Dark Ignorance our Isle o'erspread,
   Our *Musick* and our *Poetry* lay dead:
   But the dull Malice of a Barb'rous Age,
   Fell most severe on *David's* Sacred Page;
   To wound his Sense, and quench his Hev'n-born Fire,
   Three dull Translators lewdly did conspire.
   In holy Dogg'rel, and low-chiming Prose,
   The King and Poet they at once Depose.
   Vainly he did th'unrighteous Change bemoan,
   And languish'd in vile Numbers not his own:
   Nor stop'd his Usage here ——
   For what escap'd in *Wisdom's* ancient Rhimes,
   Was murder'd o'er and o'er by the *Composer's Chimes*.

   What Praises, *Purcell*, to thy Skill are due;
   Who hast to *Judah's* Monarch been so True?
   By thee he moves our Hearts, by thee he Reigns,
   By thee shakes off his old Inglorious Chains,
   And sees new Honours done to his Immortal Strains.
   Not *Italy*, the Mother of each Art,

Did e'er a Juster, Happier Son impart.
In thy Performance we with Wonder find
Bassani's Genius to *Corelli's* joy'nd.
Sweetness combin'd with Majesty, prepares
To raise Devotion with Inspiring Airs.

Thus I unknown my Gratitude express,
And conscious Gratitude could pay no less.
This Tribute from each *British Muse* is due,
Our whole Poetic Tribe's oblig'd to you.
For where the Author's Scanty Words have fail'd,
Your happier Graces, *Purcell*, have prevail'd.
And surely none but you with equal Ease
Could add to *David*, and make *Durfy* please.[6]

> The two volumes of *Harmonia Sacra* were a big publishing
> enterprise. After the coronation of William and Mary there
> was a marked increase in the number of small publishing and
> pedagogical projects with which Purcell was involved. This
> undoubtedly reflected his growing reputation, but another
> factor was the changes that music at court underwent at this
> time. Some of them were due to a need for economy and
> others to William's Calvinism, but the net result was a general
> retrenchment of the musical establishment. Purcell's song-
> writing activities expanded, and he produced independent
> compositions as well as instrumental music for plays. The
> pieces began to appear in published collections. As Henry
> Playford wrote in '*An Advertisement to the Reader*' in *Deliciae
> Musicae*:

*MY design in this new Collection of MUSICK is to give the World the best
Entertainment I can of that kind. What I publish is from Dr. Blow's, Mr.
Purcell's, and other Eminent Masters Composition; the SONGS will commend
themselves, and my Undertaking will be justify'd by them. I shall continue to
make my Collection, and publish it every Term, so that nothing will be old
before it comes to your Hands; and you shall always have a new Entertainment
prepar'd, before you have lost the Relish of the former,*

By your Servant,
H.P.[7]

During these years Purcell must have begun his revisions of John Playford's *Breefe Introduction to the Skill of Musick*. This had first been published in 1654, and by 1660 was in its third edition. Playford's portrait appeared as a frontispiece, to which was appended the following short verse, expressing his ideals behind the project.

> *This, PLAYFORD'S Shadow doth present,*
> *Peruse his Book and there you'le see*
> *His whole Designe is Publique Good*
> *His Soule and Minde an Harmonie.*[8]

Playford enlarged upon the ideals in his lengthy foreword (which is mainly given over to the biblical justification for the learning of music), but near the end we receive a glimpse of his view of domestic music-making in England in the second half of the seventeenth century.

Those who are Lovers *hereof, must allow* Musick *to be the Gift of God; yet, like others his* Graces *and* Benefits, *is not given to the Idle; those that desire to have it, must reach it to them with the hand of Industry, by putting in practise the* Works *and* Inventions *of* skilful Artists, Books *of* Instructions to Musick, *our* Nation *is not so well stored as* Forrein Countries *are; what have been printed in this Nation worthy of perusal are only two, viz. Mr.* Morley's Introduction, *&* Mr. *Butler's Principles of Musick, both which are very rare and scarce to be had, the Impressions of them being long since sold off; I have therefore in a* Brief *and* Easie *method set down the whole* Grounds *of Musick, which are necessary for* young Practitioners, *both for* Song *and* Viol. *I confess, men better able than my self might have spared my pains, but their Slowness and Modesty (being as I conceive unwilling to appear in Print about so small a matter) have put me upon the* Work, *which I count very useful, though with the danger of not being so well done as they might have performed it. The* Rules *of all Arts ought to be delivered in* plain *and* brief *Language, and not with* flowers *of* Eloquence, *and so this* Work *is more suitable to my* Abilities. *The* Work *as it is, I must confess, is not all my own, some part thereof was Collected out of other mens* Works, *which I hope will the more Commend it; and if the* Brevity, Plainness, *and* Usefulness *thereof may beget any acceptance with thee, it will encourage me to do thee more service in other things of this nature.*

                                                    Thine
                                                John Playford.[9]

Henry Playford kept many of his father's projects alive. He printed the eleventh edition of the *Introduction* in 1687, and commissioned Purcell to revise the third part for the edition which appeared in 1694. The title page tells us that it contains 'The Art of Descant . . . : In a more Plain and Easie Method than any heretofor Published . . . Corrected and Amended by Mr Henry Purcell'. Towards the end of this section Purcell outlines some principles of composing over a ground, the technique often used by him, most famously in Dido's lament from *Dido and Aeneas*.

One Thing that was forgot to be spoken of in its proper place, I think necessary to say a little of now, which is Composing upon a *Ground*, a very easie thing to do, and requires but little Judgment: As 'tis generally used in *Chacones*, where they regard only good Air in the *Treble*, and often the *Ground* is four Notes gradually descending, but to maintain *Fuges* upon it would be difficult, being confined like a *Canon* to a *Plain Song*. There are also pretty *Dividing Grounds*, of whom the *Italians* were the first Inventors, to Single *Songs* or *Songs* of Two Parts, which to do neatly, requires considerable Pains, and the best way to be acquainted with 'em, is to score much, and chuse the best Authors.[10]

Purcell closes with:

All that I shall further add, is to wish, That what is here mentioned may be as Useful as 'tis Intended, and then 'twill more than Recompense the Trouble of the Author.[11]

Two other projects on which Purcell must have been working at this period were the fifth edition of Edward Phillips's *New World of Words* and his own *Choice Lessons for the Harpsichord or Spinet*. Phillips's dictionary had first appeared in 1658, and was compiled with the help of experts in the main fields. In music, Dr Coleman.was a contributor to the first and second editions, John Birkenshaw and Matthew Locke to the third and fourth editions and Locke and Henry Purcell to

the fifth edition, published in 1696. Clearly Locke, who died
in 1677, can have been involved in the fifth edition only to
the extent of contributing definitions Purcell revised, or at
least approved. Some of Purcell's definitions will seem rather
obvious to us, but the additions to the new volume indicate
some interesting lacunae in earlier editions.

Anthem: a divine Song consisting of Verses sung alternatively
                by the two opposite Quires, and Chorus's.

Fantasie: a Piece of Composition full of Harmony, but which
                cannot be reduc'd under any of the regular kinds.

Pavan: a grave and majestick sort of Dance that came from
                Spain, wherein the Dancers turn round and wheel
                about one after another: also the gravest and the
                slowest sort of Instrumental Musick, consisting of
                three Strains.

Ritornello: the Repeating a Couplet of Verses at the end of a
                Stanza, or of half a dozen Notes at the end of a
                Song.

Trumpet: a Warlike Musical Instrument, in use among the
                Cavalry, and serving for the same Purposes, as the
                Drum among the Infantry.

Trumpet Marine: an Instrument with a Belly resembling a Lute, and
                a very long Neck, with one String, which being
                struck with a Hair Bow, makes a noise like a
                Trumpet.[12]

Choice Lessons for the Harpsichord or Spinet also appeared,
posthumously, in 1696, with a dedication by Frances Purcell.

To
Her Royal Highness the Princess of Denmark.

Your Highness's Generous Encouragem[t] of my deceased Husband's Perform-
ances in Musick, together with the great Honour your Highness's has don that
Science, in your Choice of that Instrument, for which the following Compo-
sitions were made; will I hope Justifie to the World, or at least excuse to your
Goodness this Presumption of Laying both them and my Self at your Highness's
Feet. This Madam is the highest Honour I can pay to his Memory; for
Certainly, it cannot be more advantageously recommended either to the Present,
or Future Age, than by your Highness's Patronage which as it was the Greatest
Ambition of his Life, so it will be the only comfort of his Death to,

> *Your Highness's most Obedient*
> *Humble Servant.*
> *Frances Purcell.* [13]

Purcell's opening instructions are fascinating because they are
addressed directly to the performer, and read like a letter
from a master to a pupil.

There will be nothing Conduce more to y[e] perfect ataining to play on y[e]
Harpsicord or Spinnet, then a serious application to y[e] following rules, In
order to which you must first learn y[e] Gamut or Scale of Musick, getting y[e]
names of y[e] notes by heart, & observing at y[e] same time what line & space
every note stands on, that you may know & distingush them at first sight, in
any of y[e] following Lessons, to which purpose I have placed a Scheme of keys
exactly as they are in y[e] Spinnet or Harpsicord. & on every key y[e] first letter
of y[e] note directing to y[e] names lines & Spaces where y[e] proper note stands.

All lessons on y[e] Harpsicord or Spinnet, are prickt on six lines, & two
staves, in score (or struck through both staves with strokes or bars Joyning
them together) y[e] first stave contains y[e] treble part, & is perform'd with y[e]
right hand, the second stave is y[e] bass and consequently play'd with y[e] left hand.
in the foregoing example of y[e] Gamut there are thirty black Keyes, which is y[e]
number contained on y[e] Spinnet or Harpsicord, but to some Harpsicords they
add to that number both above & below notes standing below y[e] six lines,
which have leger lines added to them are called double, as double CC=faut,
or double DD=sol=re, soe they are above on y[e] treble hand, but then they
are call'd in alt as being y[e] highest, there are likewise in y[e] example twenty
inward keyes, which are white they are y[e] half notes or flats and sharps to y[e]

other keyes, A sharp is mark'd thus (#) and where it is placed before any note in a Lesson it must be play'd on the inner key or half note above, which will make it sound half a note higher, a flat is marked thus (b) and where it is placed to any note it must be play'd on y^e inner key or half notes below y^e proper note, and makes it sound half a note lower, as for example the same inner key that makes A=ve Sharp does also make B mi=flat, soe that y^e half notes through=out y^e Scale are sharps to y^e plain keyes below them and flats to y^e plain keyes above them.

Example of time or length of Notes

There being nothing more difficult in Musick than playing of true time, tis therefore nessesary to be observ'd by all practitioners, of which there are two sorts, Common time, & Triple time, & is distingush'd by this C this ₵ or this Ø mark, ye first is a very slow movement, ye next a little faster, and ye last to brisk & airry time, & each of them has allways to ye length of one, Semibreif in a barr, which is to be held in playing as long as you can moderatly tell four; by saying one, two, three, four two Minums as long as one Semibreif, four Crotchets as long as two Minums, eight Quavers as long as four Crotchets, sixteen semiquavers as long as eight Quavers.

Triple time consists of either three or six Crotchets in a barr, and is to be known by this $\frac{3}{2}$ this 3 or this $\frac{6}{4}$ marke, to the first there is three Minums in a barr, and is commonly play'd very slow, [the second has three Crotchets in a barr, and they are to be play'd slow,] the third has y^e same as y^e former but is play'd faster, y^e last has six Crotchets in a barr & is Commonly to brisk tunes as Jiggs and Paspys, when there is a prick or dott following any Note it is to be held half as long again as ye Note itself is, lett it be Semibreif, Minum, Crotchet or Quaver, when you see a Semibreif rest you are to leave of playing so long as you can be in counting four; a Minum rest so long as you tell two, and a Crotchet one, and so in proportion a Quaver and Semiquaver you may know how these rests are marked in ye five lines under the example of time.[14]

These instructions end with the 'Rules for Graces', a table of ornaments which tells the harpsichord student most of what he or she would need to know to embellish a piece correctly.

Much of Purcell's ornamentation, however, was written out, particularly in the vocal works, to the extent that Charles Burney (unfairly) attributed Purcell's fall from fashion to it.

Rules for Graces

A Shake is mark'd thus [symbol] explaind thus [symbol] a beat mark'd thus [symbol] explaind thus [symbol] a plain note & shake thus [symbol] explain'd thus [symbol] a fore fall mark'd thus [symbol] explain'd thus [symbol] a back fall mark'd thus [symbol] explaind thus [symbol] a mark [for] the turn thus [symbol] explain'd thus [symbol] the mark for y[e] shake turn'd thus [symbol] explaind thus [symbol] observe that you allway's shake from the note above and beat from note or half note below, according to the key you play in, and for y[e] plain note a shake if it be a note without a point you are to hold half the quantity of it plain, and th[en] upon y[e] note above that which is mark'd and shake the other half, but if it be a no[te] with a point to it you are to hold all the note plain and shake only the point, a slur is ma[rk'd] thus [symbol] explain'd thus [symbol] the mark for y[e] battery thus [symbol] explained thus [symbol] the bass Clift mark'd thus [symbol] the Tenner Clift thus [symbol] the Treble Clift thus [symbol] a bar is mark'd thus [symbol] at y[e] end of every time that it may be the more easy to keep time, a Dou[ble] bar is mark'd thus [symbol] and set down at y[e] end of every Strain, which imports your play y[e] strain twice, a repeat is mark'd thus [symbol] and signifies you must repeat from note to y[e] end of the Strain or less on, to know what key a tune is in, observe y[e] last note Close of y[e] tune, for by that note y[e] key is nam'd, all Round O end with y[e] first strain.

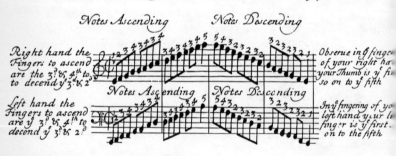

Purcell, who composed for ignorant and clumsy performers, was obliged to write down all the fashionable graces and embellishment of the times, on which account, his Music soon became obsolete and old fashioned.[15]

> *Choice Lessons for the Harpsichord* is clearly a pedagogical document and reflects the large amount of time that Purcell seems to have spent teaching during the 1680s and 1690s. Among the pupils of whom we have record is one 'Mr Hodg', who appears to have been delinquent in settling his accounts. A similar delinquency on the part of one Mr Webber inspired the following letter to the Dean of Exeter.

                     Westminster, November the 2nd, 1686

I have wrote several times to Mr. Webber concerning what was due to me on Hodg's account and received no answer, which has occasioned this presumption in giving you the trouble of a few lines relating to the matter. It is ever since the beginning of June last that the money has been due: the sum is £27, *viz.* £20 for half a year's teaching and boarding the other a bill of £7 for necessaries which I laid out for him, the bill Mr. Webber has. Compassion moves me to acquaint you of a great many debts Mr. Hodg contracted whilst in London and to some who are so poor 'twere an act of charity as well as justice to pay 'em. I hope you will be so kind as to take into your consideration and also pardon this boldness from

> Sir, your most obliged
> humble servant
> Hery Purcell[16]

In the 1690s the amount of private teaching Purcell undertook increased; this cannot simply have resulted from his need for a greater income, for his growing reputation must have made him a desirable master. Those studying with him at this time included John Weldon, Lady Rhoda Cavendish (née Cartwright) and Lady Elizabeth Howard; the two ladies were to be dedicatees of the 1697 sonatas and the first book of *Orpheus Britannicus* respectively.

Purcell must also have been occupied with court duties from time to time. We know little about his relationship with the royal household generally, and with Queen Mary in particular, though unsubstantiated claims of a sentimental attachment on the composer's side have been made. The only account we have of a personal rather than official occasion is that given by John Hawkins.

This tune was greatly admired by queen Mary, the consort of king William; and she once affronted Purcell by requesting to have it sung to her, he being present . . . Having a mind one afternoon to be entertained with music, [she] sent Mr. Gostling, then one of the chapel, and afterwards subdean of St. Paul's, to Henry Purcell and Mrs Arabella Hunt, who had a very fine voice, and an admirable hand on the lute, with a request to attend her; they obeyed her commands; Mr. Gostling and Mrs. Hunt sang several compositions of Purcell, who accompanied them on the harpsichord; at length the queen beginning to grow tired, asked Mrs. Hunt if she could not sing the old Scots ballad 'Cold and Raw,' Mrs. Hunt answered yes, and sang it to her lute. Purcell was all the while sitting at the harpsichord unemployed, and not a little nettled at the queen's preference of a vulgar ballad to his music; but seeing her majesty delighted with this tune, he determined that she should hear it upon another occasion: and accordingly in the next birthday song, viz., that for the year 1692, he composed an air to the words, 'May her bright example chace Vice in troops out of the land,' the bass whereof is the tune Cold and Raw . . .[17]

Purcell used the air (actually in 'May her blest example chase') as part of his 1692 birthday ode for the Queen, *Love's goddess sure was blind*. Its inclusion was undoubtedly a double-edged compliment: while pleasing her majesty, it was a knowing joke between the two of them. Another curious product of the Queen's pastimes was Purcell's 'knotting song'. Mary was a great knotter, a craft which was fashionable in the Low Countries and which she pursued at the risk of endangering her eyesight. Charles Sedley, the author of the text set by Purcell, turned to the image of knotting to contrast this gentle queen with James II's dangerous Catholic consort, Mary of Modena.

> Bless'd we! who from such Queens are freed,
> Who by vain Superstition led,
>   Are always telling Beads;
> But here's a Queen now, thanks to God,
> Who, when she rides in Coach abroad,
>   Is always knotting Threads.[18]

Rather than innocently celebrating a ladylike skill, Purcell may well have had quite another aim in mind. As far as Shakespeare was concerned, to knot was to copulate.

> The Fountain from which my current runs
> Or else dries up: to be descarded thence!
> Or keep it a cestern for foul toads
> To knot and gender in.[19]

In view of what we know about Purcell's light-hearted approach to such topics it is impossible to believe that such an interpretation did not occur to him. Further, it was first published in the *Gentleman's Journal* between the raucous

'Good neighbour, why', a duet for two quarrelling wives, and the passionate 'I sighed and owned my love' from *The Canterbury Guests*. 'Knotting' – strictly in the dressmaking sense – provided an effective image of stay-at-home womanhood in the anonymous poem which appeared on Mary's death in 1694.

> While our Great Queen went bravely to the dead,
> Our hero King was taken with the snivel.
> Sure Death's a Jacobite that thus bewitches
> Him to wear petticoats, and her the breeches.
> We were mistaken in the choice of our commanders;
> Will should have knotted, and Moll have gone to Flanders.[20]

NARCISSUS LUTTRELL
(1657–1732)

The Queen died from smallpox, and the progress of her disease is documented by the eccentric Narcissus Luttrell, who spent much of his life in seclusion at his house in Chelsea, devoting himself to study and his library. His *Brief Historical Relation of State Affairs from Sept. 1678 to April 1714* is not always accurate and events are often recounted with tedious detail, but some passages, such as those describing Queen Mary's last days, are particularly evocative of the reactions of both the court and the town. The first bleak notice comes in December 1694.

The queen is somewhat indisposed, and 'tis feared she will have the small pox.[21]

> She appeared to rally after the initial onslaught; there was hope for her recovery, and even the suggestion of a wrong diagnosis.

The queen was taken ill on Saturday last, and 'twas feared to be the small pox, but this morning her physitians perceived it to be the measles: she was this day prayed for in all the churches about this citty: . . . the king is so extreamly concerned at it, that he has ordered a bed in her majesties room at Kensington, and will not stir from her, but sees all things administred to her himself; there are no ill symptoms appear, but it is in a hopefull way of recovery.[22]

> Two days later, however, smallpox was confirmed; Luttrell
> gives a harrowing description of its symptoms.

We were in mighty hopes on Tuesday that the queens illnesse was only occasioned by the measles, but her majestie suddenly changing, and having a bad nights rest, the physitians found next morning there were some bad symptoms, that 'twas certainly the small pox, attended with St. Anthonies fire, which caused some blew spots; upon which a consult of 9 physitians was held, and they prescribed that her majestie should be again lett blood, and scarifyed in the forehead, to prevent the effects of St. Anthony's fire, and had diverse blisters made to keep it from her head; she rested tolerably well last night, but about 5 this morning began to grow worse, and has continued so most of the day, insomuch that her recovery is very much doubted: she took the sacrament last night and likewise this day from the hands of the archbishop of Canterbury.[23]

> After another two days he recorded:

Yesterday about one in the morning her majestie departed this life at Kensington; the king is mightily afflicted thereat, and the whole court, as also this citty, and 'tis impossible to express the general grief upon this occasion.[24]

> As usual, Luttrell does not spare us the details.

The council last night satt to consider of the best method for performing the funeral rites, which will be done privately on Monday night; her bowells are already deposited in Henry 7ths chappell, and the corpse will be removed this night to Whitehall, the withdrawing room being hung in mourning for that purpose, and the ceremony will be much after the nature of that of king Charles the 2d.

The queen had a dissolution of blood, so that it was impossible to save her life, as it appears since she was embalmed.[25]

> The preparations for the lying in state (which began on 21
> February) and the interment, continued throughout January
> and February.

His majesties upholster has orders to buy 6000 yards of black cloth for the hanging of Whitehall, Kensington, Hampton Court, and the presence chamber at Windsor; he is also to provide 400 yards of purple velvet for the kings bedding and apartment.

This day the workmen began to fitt up the banquetting house for the queen to lye in state; and sir Christopher Wrenn has orders to prepare rails from Whitehall to Westminster Abby, and the walks betwixt them to be gravelled, and the rails to be covered with black cloth.

The heralds at arms are preparing the necessaries for a publick funerall.

The princesse is to be cheif mourner, and 200 old women to walk before in mourning, and to have 40s. each; the whole charge is computed at about 100,000*l*.[26]

This afternoon the queen began to lye in state in the bedchamber, all the officers of her household attending, according to their offices, under the direction of the marquesse of Winchester, her chamberlain; and the ladies of honour also attend, 4 of whom stand about the corpse, and are releiv'd by others every half hour; upon her head lyes the crown, and over it a fine canopy; at her feet lyes the sword of state, the helmet and her arms upon a cushion, the banners and scutcheons hanging round; the state is very great, and more magnificent then can be exprest: all persons are admitted, without distinction: she is to lye so every day from 12 till 5 a clock till she is interr'd.[27]

> The Queen was buried on 5 March, and the choirs of both the Chapel and the Abbey attended. The Duke of Norfolk lists the order of the procession:

Proceedings to the Interrment after the Sermon.
The Queen's State

The Queen's Master of the Horse		The Queen's Lord Chamberlain
	The Church of *Westminster*, and both Choirs.	
The 3 Supporters of the Pall	The Body	The 3 Supporters of the Pall
Supporter to the Chief Mourner		Supporter to the Chief Mourner
Supporter to the Train		Supporter to the Train

Vice Chamberlain
Ladies Assistants.
Maid of Honour.
Bed-Chamber Women.
Gentlemen Pensioners to the Chapel Door.

Some Yeomen of the Guard to keep the door.[28]

Among the music by Purcell performed on this solemn
occasion was the anthem *Thou knowest, Lord, the secrets of our
hearts*. Thomas Tudway, when discussing music suitable for
devotion, give us an account of the funeral and praises this
anthem,

compos'd by Mr. Henry Purcell, after ye old way; and sung at ye interrment of Queen Mary in Westminster Abbey; a great Queen, and
extremely Lamented, being there to be interr'd, ev'ry body present, was
dispos'd, and serious, at so solemn a Service, as indeed they ought to be
at all parts of divine Worship; I appeal to all y^t were present, as well
such as understood Music, as those y^t did not, whither, they ever heard
anything, so rapturously fine, so solemn, and so Heavenly, in ye Operation, wch drew tears from all; and yet a plain Naturall Composition,
wch shews ye pow'r of Music, when 'tis rightly fitted and Adapted to
devotional purposes.[29]

VI

Purcell on the stage

DIDO AND AENEAS

Although the date and location of the première of Purcell's small masque *Dido and Aeneas* remains a matter for speculation, it seems certain that a performance of the piece was given at Josiah Priest's school in Chelsea in 1689. Mrs A. Buck, writing to her friend Mary Clarke, wife of Edward Clarke of Chipley, Somerset, mentions an opera at the school which may well be Purcell's.

Dear Madam,

Mr Clark hath bin so kind oft to call upon us; but really I have never had the good fortune to see him but once; & then in a mixt company. The Lady Hatton hath bin with us these six weeks; she came up much indisposed, but will return I hope much better. Lett my hurry be never so great, I will neglect no request of yours; I have inquired with the same care as for my self; but I can give you little satisfaction. I went my self to three schoolls. Preists att Little Chelsey was one which was much commended; but he hath lately had an Opera, which I'me sure hath done him a great injury; & Parents of the Children not satisfied with so Publick a show. I was att Hackney att one of their Balls: I cannot commend itt. Kingsinton was commended for a delicate air, but I cannot finde out what the children are improved in. Att present all schoolls are redicul'd: they have latly made a Play cal'd The Boarding School. I finde the way that the Ladys now take that live in the country, when they're come to town, they have masters home to them every day, wch they say, give them a better mean. Once a year all Ladys see our town with their offsprings. Mrs Peck & her two Daughters left town this week. They inquired most hartly after you & yours & so doth all your old acquaintance. Sr Chris: Hatton, his Lady, & self & the rest of my young ones sends humble services. The Post will be gon: I can say no more but that I am sincerely yours,

A. Buck

When you see Mr Clark pray all our services to him.[1]

For the performance at Priest's school Thomas D'Urfey (compiler of the famous collection *Wit and Mirth, or Pills to Purge Melancholy*) provided the female pupils with an occasional

epilogue justifying their sequestered education, their staging
of an all-sung opera and any immaturities in their 'tuning'.

ALL that we know the Angels do above,
I've read, is that they Sing and that they love,
The Vocal part we have tonight perform'd,
And if by Love our Hearts not are yet warn'd
Great Providence has still more bountious been
To save us from these grand Deceivers, Men,
Here blest with Innocence, and peace of Mind, ⎫
Not only bred to Virtue, but inclin'd;   ⎬
We flowrish, and defie all human kind.   ⎭
Arts curious Garden thus we learn to know,
And here secure from nipping Blasts we grow,
Let the vain Fop range o'er yon vile lewd Town,
Learn Play-house Wit, and vow 'tis all his own;
Let him Cock, Huff, Strut, Ogle, Lye, and Swear,
How he's admir'd by such and such a Player;
All's one to us, his Charms have here no power,
Our Hearts have just the Temper as before;
Besides, to shew we live with strictest Rules,
Our Nunnery-Door, is charm'd to shut out Fools;
No Love-toy here can pass to private view,
Nor *China* orange cramm'd with Billet dew,
Rome may allow strange Tricks to please her Sons,
But we are Protestants and *English* Nuns;
Like nimble Fawns, and Birds that bless the Spring
Unscar'd by turning Times we dance and sing;
We hope to please, but if some Critick here
Fond of his Wit, designs to be severe,
Let not his Patience, be worn out too soon;
In a few years we shall be all in Tune.[2]

Purcell's opera inspired one of George Bernard Shaw's most
entertaining – if politically incorrect – reviews. The show
was to be given in Bow in the East End of London. Shaw
(1856–1950) refused to believe that London existed outside the
West End, but he was so infuriated that the tickets would

therefore be given to his supposedly ignorant rival 'Musigena' (Ernest Belfort Bax) that he snatched them from his editor's desk, armed himself with a revolver and took the train out east.

When I got into the concert room I was perfectly dazzled by the appearance of the orchestra. Nearly all the desks for the second violins were occupied by ladies; beautiful young ladies. Personal beauty is not the strong point of West End orchestras, and I thought the change an immense improvement until the performance began, when the fair fiddlers rambled from bar to bar with a certain sweet indecision that had a charm of its own, but was not exactly what Purcell and Handel meant. When I say that the performance began, I do not mean to imply that it began punctually. The musicians began to drop in about ten minutes past eight, and the audience were inclined to remonstrate; but an occasional apology from the conductor, Mr F. A. W. Docker, kept them in good humor.

Dido and Eneas is 200 years old, and not a bit the worse for wear. I daresay many of the Bowegians thought that the unintentional quaintnesses of the amateurs in the orchestra were Purcellian antiquities. If so, they were never more mistaken in their lives. Henry Purcell was a great composer: a very great composer indeed; and even this little boarding-school opera is full of his spirit, his freshness, his dramatic expression, and his unapproached art of setting English speech to music. The Handel Society did not do him full justice: the work, in fact, is by no means easy; but the choir made up bravely for the distracting dances of the string quartet. Eneas should not have called Dido Deedo, any more than Juliet should call Romeo Ro-*may*-oh, or Othello call his wife Days-*day*-mona. If Purcell chose to pronounce Dido English fashion, it is not for a Bow-Bromley tenor to presume to correct him. Belinda, too, was careless in the matter of time. She not only arrived after her part had been half finished by volunteers from the choir, but in Oft She Visits she lost her place somewhat conspicuously. An unnamed singer took Come away, fellow sailors, come away: that salt sea air that makes you wonder how anyone has ever had the face to compose another sailor's song after it. I quote the concluding lines, and wish I could quote the incomparably jolly and humorous setting –

> Take a bowsy short leave of your nymphs on the shore;
> And silence their mourning
> With vows of returning,

Though never intending to visit them more.

SAILORS (*greatly tickled*). Though never – !
OTHER SAILORS (*ready to burst with laughter*). Though never – !
ALL (*uproariously*). Inte-en-ding to vi-sit them more.

I am sorry to have to add that the Handel choir, feeling that they were nothing if not solemn, contrived to subdue this rousing strain to the decorum of a Sunday school hymn; and it missed fire accordingly.[3]

> The composer Gustav Holst (1874–1934) was employed as music critic for the *Athenaeum* at the time of the Purcell bicentenary performance of *Dido and Aeneas* at the Lyceum Theatre under Charles Villiers Stanford. Stanford was criticized by many for his re-scoring of the opera and defended himself in print in later numbers of the *Athenaeum*. Holst, a former pupil of Stanford, was a staunch supporter of the older man's performance.

The Purcell *in memoriam* performances commenced too late for us to notice the most important of them this week; but a few words may be said concerning the interpretation of 'Dido and Aeneas' by pupils of the Royal College of Music on Wednesday afternoon. There seems to be considerable doubt as to when the opera was actually composed and first produced; but it is certain that it was performed in 1680 'at Mr. Josias Priest's Boarding School at Chelsey by young gentlewomen.' It has been given more than once in recent years on the concertroom platform, so that the music need not be minutely criticized again. Though, as a very early work and written for girls, it is not fully representative of Purcell's genius, it contains some characteristic music, the finest number being Dido's death song, which may be regarded as a sort of foreshadowing of Wagner's in 'Tristan und Isolde.' The libretto, by Nahum Tate, is the most wretched balderdash, and would promptly be rejected by any composer of the present day who respected his art. Much pains had been taken in the preparation of the Lyceum revival. Mr. Richard Temple and Mr. B. Soutten were responsible for the stage arrangements, and the mounting for the most part may be described as exceedingly tasteful. The additional accompaniments of Dr. Charles Wood are written with musicianly skill and discretion. Those who assert that only a harpsichord and a quartet of strings should have been used mean practically that works of the seventeenth century should be placed on the shelf. For Prof. Villiers Stanford, who conducted, we have nothing but praise, and it is worthy of note that the orchestra consisted entirely of past and present pupils of the College.[4]

> It is always possible that Holst changed his mind about Tate, for his daughter Imogen, an Aldeburgh figure and founder of the Purcell Singers, later wrote a piece defending the librettist.
>
> The famous opinionated tartness of the conductor and impresario Thomas Beecham (1879–1961) colours his short discussion of Purcell's opera, but does not negate his perceptive comments on the difficulties of staging this deceptively simple piece. He describes it as

something which may be played by a gifted company of musical amateurs or mellow professional singers for their own amusement. It is absolutely the last thing in the world to give to a company of unsophisticated students. One does not engage as leader-writer on a paper a man who is able to write only in the style of Chaucer. The manager of a concert society would never dream of engaging a pianist to play, say the Grieg Concerto, who had spent his time practising on the spinet. How, then, in the name of goodness, can anyone expect a singer to be engaged for any opera written during the last fifty or hundred years who has been brought up exclusively on such toast-and-water musical fare as *Dido and Aeneas?*[5]

> The scholar and critic Roger Savage (b. 1935) has made a distinguished contribution to Purcell studies, and he produced one of the first complete performances of *The Fairy-Queen* since the original staging. For a production of *Dido and Aeneas* in 1990 he was commissioned by New Chamber Opera to write an occasional prologue. The piece he provided reflects some of the scholarly discussion over the circumstances of the opera's first performance.

A *Prologue* to the Theatrical Masque of DIDO AND AENEAS (compos'd by Mr TATE and Mr PURCELL)

for its Representation at New College in Oxford

under the Care of Mr BURDEN

Anno 1990

Spoken by the WARDEN

Friends, I'll not vex you with a lengthy Homily:
A Prologue to an *Op'ra's* an Anomaly
In these rush'd times; and since we have in view
To offer you not one tonight but *two*,
Mine shall be brief. 'Tis said of *Tate* and *Purcell*
That they design'd, nay brought to a Rehearsal
A fine *sung* Prologue to sad *Dido's* Story
And then mislaid the Score. But Doctor *Laurie*
(In some *Van Meegeren*-blest Forger's Back-room)
Has thereof made an honest *Simulacrum*
Which shall be sung ere long. With her Complicity
We may e'en glimpse (who knows?) fair AUTHENTICITY:
That *Shangri-La*, that long'd-for Holy Grail,
That Golden Fleece, to seek which most set sail
Only to split upon some rock. E'en with her Prologue
We may be hol'd by some *malapropos* log
And *sink with all hands*! Nay, we must confess,
Hearing his Masque announc'd at the Address,
Purcell himself might rise with ireful brow
And break an oath and cry: *Gadzookers, how*
Can New Coll. Oxon. *play my* Dido *when*
Sure 'tis a mere Monastery – all Men!
Must Queen, must dear Belinda, *must the Witches*
Be sung by Lubbers hot from cricket *pitches?*
How coarse! How un-authentick! We reply:
First look, Sir, at the Beam in your own eye.
You claim (or your old Scholiasts claim at least)
Your *Op'ra* was first play'd* (*per* one *Jo. Priest*)
By an Establishment of well-bred *Lasses*!
How many of them, pray, were Tenors, Basses,
Sailor-lads, *Trojan* heroes? None, of course.
Some *secret fellows* (in a Wooden Horse)
Were spirited into that Nunnery

To make your *Opera* S. A. T. B.
But *New Coll.* scorns such Prestidigitation.
Monastick? Faugh! Benign *CO: EDUCATION*
Has spread a Decade's charms o'er *Quad* and Hall.
Our songsters here are both *authentick* all
And quite within the Statutes of a College
Where nothing's done without the *Warden's* knowledge.
Each *belle* here is a *belle*; each *beau* a *beau*.
And so – one Prologue down and one to go –
'On yon imaginary curtain, pull!' Begin the Show!

**Post-scriptum 1994*

'*First* play'd'? Some Learned Wits of late have thought
That Precedence is owing to the Court,
That th' *Opr'a* as a *Whitehall* dish begun
Before it dwindled to a *Chelsey-bun*.[6]

THEATRE MUSIC OF THE 1690s

The founder and, for the most part, author of the *Gentleman's Journal*, Pierre Motteux was a Frenchman who had come to London after the revocation of the Edict of Naples. He undertook a range of journalistic activities, completed Urquhart's translation of Rabelais and made an English version of Cervantes' *Don Quixote*. An announcement from his periodical illustrates one of the many ways songs reached the public.

You have here the two new Songs which I promised to send you every Month: The first is set by Mr. *Purcell*, to whom I must own my self doubly obliged; for he hath not only made the Notes extremely fine, but nicely adapted them to my Words.[7]

The song in question was 'Stript of their green appear'. More than a dozen of Purcell's songs were printed in Motteux's *Gentleman's Journal* during the 1690s, with texts by Congreve, Southerne, Tate and others. Some were undoubtedly written for the *Journal*, while others were occasional pieces (such as 'Sawney is a bonny lad', which was 'Sung at the Entertainment for Prince *Louis* of *Baden*' in 1694) or came from plays (for example 'The danger is over' from Southerne's *Fatal Marriage*).

The incidental music for *Amphitryon* was the first collaboration between Purcell and the playwright John Dryden (1631–1700). Dryden had been active as a dramatist and poet for some time, having published his well-known *Annus Mirabilis* in 1667; he became Poet Laureate in 1668 and Historiographer Royal in 1670. When praising the composer Grabu for his score for *Albion and Albanius* of 1685, Dryden had been dismissive of English composers, and yet on 24 October 1690 he was writing the following.

But what has been wanting on my Part, has been abundantly supplyed by the Excellent Composition of Mr. *Purcell*; in whose Person we have at length found an *English-man*, equal with the best abroad. At least my Opinion of him has been such, since his happy and judicious Performances in the late *Opera* [almost certainly *Dioclesian*]; and the Experience I have had of him, in the setting of my Three Songs for this *Amphitryon*.[8]

> Roger North's remarks on Purcell's operas are a mixed bag of prejudice and a desire for Italian opera *à la* Cavalli. Indeed, so desirous was he for all-sung operas that he invented the term 'semi-opera', a description which has haunted Purcell's works ever since.

It had bin strange if the gentlemen of the Theatres had sate still all this while [during the expansion of 'Publick musick meetings'], seeing as they say a pudding creep, that is a violent inclination in the Towne to follow musick, and they not serve themselves of it. Therefore M⟨r⟩ Betterton who was the cheif ingineer of the stage, contrived a sort of plays, which were called Operas but had bin more properly styled Semioperas, for they consisted of half Musick, and half Drama. The cheif of these were *Circe*, *The Fayery Queen*, *Dioclesian* and *King Arthur*; which latter was composed by Purcell and is unhappyly lost. These were followed at first; but by an error of mixing 2 capitall enterteinements, could not stand long. For some that would come to the play, hated the musick, and others that were very desirous of the musick, would not bear the interruption that so much rehearsall gave, so that it is best to have either by it self intire.[9]

An overview of Purcell's operatic activities during this period

is given by the chronicler John Downes (?–1712), a somewhat
enigmatic figure about whose age and career we know little.
He produced the remarkable *Roscius Anglicanus*, and supplied
us with the nearest thing we have to a contemporary review
of the operas.

King Arthur an Opera, wrote by Mr. *Dryden*; it was Excellently Adorn'd
with Scenes and Machines: The Musical Part set by Famous Mr. *Henry
Purcel*; and Dances made by Mr. *Jo. Priest*: The Play and Musick pleas'd
the Court and City, and being well perform'd, twas very Gainful to the
Company.

   The Prophetess, or Dioclesian an Opera, wrote by Mr. *Betterton*; being
set out with Coastly Scenes, Machines and Cloaths: The Vocal and Instrumental Musick, done by Mr. *Purcel*; and Dances by Mr. *Priest*; it gratify'd
the Expectation of Court and City; and got the Author great Reputation.

   The Fairy Queen, made into an Opera, from a Comedy of Mr. *Shakespears*; This in Ornaments was Superior to the other Two; especially in
Cloaths, for all the Singers and Dancers, Scenes, Machines and Decorations, all most profusely set off; and excellently perform'd, chiefly the
Instrumental and Vocal part. Compos'd by the said Mr. *Purcel*, and
Dances by Mr. *Priest*. The Court and Town were wonderfully satisfy'd
with it; but the Expences in setting it out being so great, the Company
got very little by it.[10]

DIOCLESIAN

Purcell set the lyrics and provided the dance music for the
adaptation of Massinger's and Fletcher's *Prophetess* by Thomas
Betterton (*c.* 1635–1710), also known as *The History of Dioclesian*. It was the first of his dramatic operas or semi-operas to
reach the stage. Purcell is named as the author of the dedication to the published score, which, the *London Gazette*
revealed, could be had by subscription from John Carr or
Henry Playford.

The Vocal and Instrumental Musick, in the Opera, called, The Prophetess, Composed by Mr Henry Purcell, is design'd to be Printed by way
of Subscriptions. Proposals may be seen at Mr. John Carr's Shop in the

Middle-Temple-Gate, and at Mr. Henry Playford's Shop, near the Inner-Temple Church, who are appointed to take Subscriptions.[11]

> Purcell seems to have lost out on the whole deal in the end,
> for he included the following advertisement at the back of
> the published score.

Advertisement

IN order to the speedier Publication of this Book, I employed two several Printers; but One of them falling into some trouble, and the Volume swelling to a Bulk beyond my expectation, have been the Occasions of this Delay.

It has been objected that some of the Songs are already common; but I presume that the Subscribers, upon perusal of the Work, will easily be convinc'd that they are not the Essential Parts of it.

I have, according to my Promise in the Proposals, been very carefull in the Examination of every Sheet, and hope the Whole will appear as Correct as any yet Extant.

My desire to make it as cheap as possibly I cou'd to the Subscribers, prevail'd with me so far above the consideration of my own Interest, that I find, too late, the Subscription-money will scarcely amount to the Expence of compleating this Edition.[12]

> Although attributed to Henry Purcell, the manuscript of the
> epistle to the score is in Dryden's hand; Purcell surely had
> some say in it, but it is likely that Dryden was its author.
> Roswell G. Ham's edition of the epistle is quoted below. The
> portions of the original draft that were omitted in publication
> are set in italic. The parentheses round text in italic show
> crossed-out alternatives in the manuscript draft, while those
> round text in ordinary type show alternatives that appear in
> the published version.

YOUR Grace [Charles, Duke of Somerset] has been pleasd, so particularly to favour the Composition of the Musique in Diocletian, that from thence I have *this* been incouraged to this presumption of dedicating not onely it, but (also) the unworthy Authour of it, to your protection. All arts and Sciences have had their first encouragement from great persons; and owe their propagation and success to their *favour* (esteeme): like some sort of fruit trees, which being of a tender constitution, and delicate in their nature, require*d* the shadow of the Cedar to shield their Infancy, from *Stormes* (blites) and Tempests. Musick and poetry have ever been acknowledgd Sisters, which walking hand in hand, support (& *grace*) each other: *And* As poetry is (*illeg.*) the harmony of words, so musick is that of notes: and as poetry is a rise above prose and oratory, so is Musick the exaltation of poetry. Both of them may excell apart, but sure they are most excellent when they are joind, because *then*, nothing is (then) wanting to either of their perfections: for *then* thus they appeare, like wit & beauty in the same person. *Painting is, indeed, another sister, being like them, an Imitation of Nature: but I may venture to say she is a dumb Lady, whose charmes are onely to the eye: a Mute actour upon the stage, who can neither be heard nor read there, nor read afterwards. Besides, that she is a single piece; to be seen onely in one place, at once: but the other two, can propagate their species; and as many printed (or written) copyes as there are of a poem or a* pie *composition of Musick, in so many severall places (at the same time), the poem & the Musick, may be read, & practisd, and admir'd. Thus painting is a confin'd, & solitary Art, the other two are as it were in consort, & diffus'd through the world; partakeing somewhat of the Nature of the* Divinity (*Deity*), *which at once is in all places. This is not sayd in disparagement of that noble Art; but onely to give the due precedence, to the* others, *which are more noble; and which are of nearer kindred to the soule; have less of the matter, & more of the forme; less of the manuall operation, & more of the* rationall *spirituall part, in* our *humane nature. Yet let it allwayes be acknowledgd, that painting and Statuary can express both our actions & our passions: that if they neither speake nor move, they seem to do both: and if they impose on the eye, yet they deceive nobly: when they make shadows pass for substances, and even animate the brass & marble. But* poetry and painting have arriv'd to their perfection in our own Country: Musick, is yet but (*illeg.*) in its Nonage: a *prattling foreign* forward child which *rather* gives hope of what it may be herafter in England, *than what it has produc'd already hetherto produc'd* (when the Masters of it shall find more encouragement). Tis now learning Italian, which is its best Master; and studying *somewhat* (a little) of the French ayre, to give it somewhat more of gayety and fashion. *Thus being* farther from the sun, we are of later growth, than our Neighbor Countryes; and must be content, to shake off our barbarity by degrees; *and leave the hedge notes of our homely Ancestours.* The present age seemes already disposd to be refind: and to distinguish betwixt wild fancy, and a just, numerous composition. *Thus* (So) far, the Genius (*and example*) of your Grace, has already prevaild on *them* (us): Many of the Nobility and Gentry, have followed your Illustrious Example in this *encouragement* (protection) of Musick. Nay even our Poets *grow* begin to grow ashamd, of their harsh*ness* & broken Numbers: and promise to file our uncouth Language, into smoother words. *For, by their pardon, I may be bold to* tell them (*say*) *that hetherto they have not enough considerd, the sweetness & Majesty of Sound: and that the little paines which they have employd on their ragged verses, has been the occasion of our great* trouble *labour & trouble in the composition of them. And therefore I will presume to tell them*, once for all, *that* if they *he who has not (naturally) a good eare, is not* very (*over*) *fit for his own trade, but is a very judgment and Flayle to ours. But I am too sensible of my own imperfections to expose the failings of other men, in an Art, which I pretend not to understand; at least not more than Nature teaches me, to abhorre the grateing of unharmonious sounds.* Once more therefore I presume, to *dedicate* (offer) my selfe, & this present composition (with all humility) to your Graces favour, & protection; at least, till I can redeeme so meane a present by *offering you* one which may better deserve your acceptation. Be pleasd to pardon my Ambition, which had no other meanes to obtaine the honour of being made known to you, but onely this. The Toun, which has been so indulgent to my first endeavours in this kind, has encouraged *my* me to proceed in the same attempt, and Your *Graces acceptance of* (favour to) this trifle, will be a good omen (not onely) to the *next* success of the next, but (also) to all the future performances of

> Your Graces most obediant
> & most Obliged Servant
> Henry Purcell[13]

The opera was preceded by a prologue, a piece which was considered so partisan that it had to be withdrawn; not only was it omitted after the first performance, but it was pulled from all but the very earliest editions. There can be no doubt of the anti-Williamite line of its commentary on wealth and war and theatrical feuding, which the compliment to Queen Mary in the last line was clearly not enough to offset. One wonders how much Purcell shared Dryden's sentiments.

PROLOGUE
TO THE

PROPHETESS
Written by Mr. DRYDEN.
Spoken by Mr. BETTERTON.

What Nostradame, *with all his Art can guess*
The Fate of our approaching Prophetess?
A Play which like a Prospective set right,
Presents our vast Expences close to sight;
But turn the Tube, and there we sadly view
Our distant gains; and those uncertain too.
A sweeping Tax, which on our selves we raise;
And all like you, in hopes of better days.
When will our Losses warn us to be wise!
Our Wealth decreases, and our Charges rise:
Money the sweet Allurer of our hopes,
Ebbs out in Oceans, and comes in by Drops.
We raise new Objects to provoke delight;
But you grow sated e're the second sight.
False Men, even so, you serve your Mistresses;
They rise three Storys, in their towring dress;
And after all, you love not long enough,
To pay the Rigging, e're you leave 'em off.
Never content, with what you had before;
But true to Change, and English *Men all ore.*
New Honour calls you hence; and all your Care
Is to provide the horrid pomp of War:
In Plume and Scarf, Jack-boots and Bilbo Blade
Your Silver goes, that should support our Trade.
Go unkind Hero's, leave our Stage to mourn,
Till rich from vanquish'd Rebels you return;
And the fat Spoyls of Teague *in Tryumph draw,*
His Firkin-Butter, and his Usquebaugh.
Go Conquerors of your Male and Female Foes;
Men without Hearts, and Women without Hose.
Each bring his Love, a Bogland Captive home,
Such proper Pages, will long Trayns become:
With Copper-Collars, and with brawny Backs,
Quite to put down the Fashion of our Blacks.

Then shall the pious Muses pay their Vows,
And furnish all their Lawrels for your brows;
Their tuneful Voice shall rise for your delights;
We want not Poets fit to sing your fights.
But you bright Beauties, for whose only sake,
These doughty Knights such dangers undertake,
When they with happy Gales are gone away, ⎫
With your propitious Presence grace our Play; ⎬
And with a sigh, their empty seats survey. ⎭
Then think on that bare Bench my Servant sate;
I see him Ogle still, and hear him Chat:
Selling facetious Bargains, and propounding
That witty Recreation, call'd Dum-founding.
Their Loss with patience, we will try to bear;
And wou'd do more to see you often here.
That our Dead Stage, Reviv'd by your fair eyes,
Under a Female Regency may rise. [14]

However, we learn from the *Muses Mercury* of 1707 – written
in the reign of Queen Anne – that jealousy and politics would
seem to have motivated those involved.

This Prologue was forbidden to be spoken the second Night of the Representation of the *Prophetess*. Mr. *Shadwell* was the occasion of its being
taken notice of by the Ministry in the last Reign: He happen'd to be at the
House on the first Night, and taking the beginning of the Prologue to have
a *double Meaning*, and that Meaning to reflect on the *Revolution*, he told a
Gentleman, *He would immediately put a stop to it*. When that Gentleman
ask'd, Why he wou'd do the Author such a Disservice? He said, *Because
while Mr.* Dryden *was Poet Laureat, he wou'd never let any Play of his be
Acted*. Mr. *Shadwell* informing the Secretary of State of it, and representing it in its worst Colours, the Prologue was never Spoken afterwards, and is
not Printed in Mr. *Dryden's* Works, or his Miscellanies. Whatever was the
meaning of the Author then, had he liv'd to have seen the Happy Effects of
the Revolution in Her present Majesty's Triumphant Reign, he wou'd
have blush'd at his Poor Politicks, and Vain Malice. Tho' we say this with
some warmth, we wou'd not be understood to mean any thing derogatory
to Mr. *Dryden's* Merit; to which, as a Poet, we pay as much deference as

any one, and think the *British* Muse indebted to him for his admirable Versification, as much as to all the Writers who went before him.[15]

KING ARTHUR

Dryden's epistle dedicatory to *King Arthur* claims that his script had been written several years before and that much had been reworked, so as 'not to offend the present Times, nor a Government which has hitherto protected me', and also to accommodate Henry Purcell's wishes as a word setter. In 1684, at the time of the first writing, the lyrics were probably to have been set by Louis Grabu. Dryden revised the text – just how extensively is unknown – for Purcell after the success of *Dioclesian*, and apparently believed that the resultant work was better than what he had originally intended, at least in its musical sections. The epistle is interesting evidence of Purcell's insisting on his rights when collaborating with even so eminent a poet as Dryden.

To the
MARQUISS of HALLIFAX

My *LORD*,

THIS Poem was the last Piece of Service, which I had the Honour to do, for my Gracious Master King CHARLES the Second: And, though he liv'd not to see the Performance of it on the Stage; yet the PRO-LOGUE to it, which was the *Opera* of *Albion* and *Albanius*, was often practis'd before Him at *Whitehal*, and encourag'd by His Royal Appro-bation. It was indeed a Time, which was proper for Triumph, when He had overcome all those Difficulties which for some Years had perplex'd His Peaceful Reign: But when He had just restor'd His People to their Senses, and made the latter End of His Government, of a Piece with the Happy Beginning of it, He was on the suddain snatched away, from the Blessings and Acclamations of His Subjects, who arriv'd so late to the Knowledge of Him, that they had but just time enough to desire him longer, before they were to part with Him for ever. Peace be with the Ashes of so Good a King! Let His Humane Frailties be forgotten; and His Clemency and Moderation (the inherent Virtues of His Family) be remembered with a Grateful Veneration by Three Kingdoms, through which He spread the Blessings of them. And, as your Lordship held a principal Place in His Esteem, and perhaps the first in His Affection, during His latter Troubles; the Success which accompanied those prudent Counsels, cannot but reflect an Honour on those few who manag'd them; and wrought out, by their Faithfulness and Diligence, the Public Safety. I might dilate on the Difficulties which attended that Undertaking, the Temper of the People, the Power, Arts and Interest of the contrary Party, but those are all of them Invidious Topicks; they are too green in our Remembrance; and he who touches on them *Incedit per ignes, suppositos cineri doloso*. But, without reproaching one side to praise another, I may justly recommend to both, those wholsom Counsels, which wisely administered, and as well executed, were the Means of preventing a Civil War, and of extinguishing a growing Fire which was just ready to have broken forth among us. So many Wives, who have yet their Husbands in their Arms; so many Parents, who have not the Number of their Children lessen'd; so many Villages, Towns and Cities, whose Inhabitants are not decreas'd, their Property violated, or their Wealth diminish'd, are yet owing to the sober Conduct, and happy Results of your Advice. If a true Account may be expected by future Ages, from the present, your Lordship will be delivered over to Prosperity, in a fairer Character than I have given: And be read, not in the Preface of a Play, (whose Author is not vain enough to promise Immortality to others, or to hope it for himself) but in many Pages of a Chronicle, fill'd with Praises of your Administration. For if Writers be just to the Memory of King *CHARLES* the Second, they cannot deny him to have been an exact Knower of Mankind, and a perfect distinguisher of their talents. 'Tis true, his Necessities often forc'd him to vary his Councellours and Councils, and sometimes to employ such Persons in the Management of his Affairs, who were rather fit for his present purpose, than satisfactory to his Judgment: But where it was Choice in him, not Compulsion, he was Master of too much good Sense to delight in heavy Conversation; and whatever his Favourites of State might be, yet those of his Affection, were Men of Wit. He was easie with these; and comply'd only with the former: But in the latter part of his Life, which certainly requir'd to be most cautiously manag'd, his secret Thoughts were communicated but to few; and those selected of that sort, who were *Amici omnium Honorarum*, able to advise him in a serious Consult, where his Honour and Safety were concern'd; and afterwards capable of entertaining him with pleasant Discourse, as well as profitable. In this Maturest part of his Age, when he had been long season'd with Difficulties and Dangers, and was grown to a Niceness in his Choice, as being satisfied how few cou'd be trusted: and, of those who cou'd be trusted, how few cou'd serve him, he confined himself to a small Number of Bosom Friends; amongst whom, the World is much mistaken, if your Lordship, was not the first.

If the Rewards which you receiv'd for those Services, were only Honours, it rather shew'd the Necessities of the Times, than any want of Kindness in your Royal Master: And as the Splendour of your Fortune stood not in need of being supported by the Crown, so likewise, in being satisfied without other Recompence, you show'd your self to be above a Mercenary Interest; and strengthen'd that Power, which bestowed those Titles on you: Which truly speaking, were Marks of Acknowledgement more than Favour.

But, as a Skilful Pilot will not be tempted out to Sea, in suspected Weather, so have you wisely chosen to withdraw yourself from publick Business, when the Face of Heaven grew troubled; and the frequent shifting of the Winds foreshew'd a storm: There are Times and Seasons when the best Patriots are willing to withdraw their Hands from Commonwealth; as *Phocion* in his latter Days was observ'd to decline the Management of Affairs: Or, as *Cicero*, (to draw the Similitude more home) left the Pulpit, for *Tusculum*, and the praise of the Oratory, for the sweet Enjoyments of a private Life. And, in the Happiness of those Retirements, has more oblig'd Posterity by his *Moral Precepts*, than he did the Republick, in quelling the Conspiracy of *Catiline*. What prudent Man, wou'd not rather follow the Example of his Retreat, than stay like *Cato*, with a stubborn unseasonable Virtue, to oppose the Torrent of the People, and at last be driven from the Market-place by a Riot of a Multitude, uncapable of Counsel, and deaf to Eloquence? There is likewise a Portion of our Lives, which every Wise Man may justly reserve to his own peculiar use, and that without defrauding his Native Country. A Roman Soldier was allow'd to plead the Merit of his Services for his dismission at such an Age; and there was but one Exception to that Rule, which was, an Invasion from the *Gauls*. How far that, may work with your Lordship, I am not certain; but I hope it is not coming to the Trial.

In the mean time, while the Nation is secur'd from Foreign Attempts, by so powerful a Fleet, and we enjoy, not only the Happiness, but even the Ornaments of peace, in the Divertisement of the Town, I humbly offer you this Trifle, which if it succeed upon the Stage, is like to be the

chiefest Entertainment of our Ladies and Gentlemen this Summer. When
I wrote it, seven Years ago, I employ'd some reading about it, to inform
my self out of *Beda*, *Bochartus*, and other Authors, concerning the Rites
and Customs of the Heathen Saxons; as I also us'd the little Skill I have
in Poetry to adorn it. But not to offend the present Times, nor a Government which has hitherto protected me, I have been oblig'd so much to
alter the first Design, and take away so Many Beauties from the Writing,
that it is now no more what it was formerly, than the present Ship of the
Royal Sovereign, after so often taking down, and altering, to the Vessel it
was at the first Building. There is nothing better, than what I intended,
but the Musick; which has since arriv'd to a greater Perfection in *England*,
than ever formerly; especially passing through the Artful Hands of Mr.
Purcel, who has Compos'd it with so great a Genius, that he has nothing
to fear but an ignorant, ill-judging Audience. But the Numbers of Poetry
and Vocal Musick, are sometimes so contrary, that in many places I have
been oblig'd to cramp my Verses, and make them rugged to the Reader,
that they may be harmonious to the Hearer: Of which I have no Reason
to repent me, because these sorts of Entertainment are principally design'd
for the Ear and Eye; and therefore in Reason my Art on this occasion,
ought to be subservient to his. And besides, I flatter my self with an
Imagination, that a Judicious Audience will easily distinguish betwixt the
Songs, wherein I have comply'd with him, and those in which I have
followed the Rules of Poetry, in the Sound and Cadence of the Words.
Notwithstanding all these Disadvantages, there is a somewhat still remaining of the first Spirit with which I wrote it: And, though I can only speak
by ghess, of what pleas'd my first and best Patroness the Dutchess of
Monmouth in the reading, yet I will venture my Opinion, by the knowledge I have long had of her Grace's Excellent Judgment and true taste of
Poetry, that the parts of the Airy and Earthy Spirits, and that Fairy kind
of writing, which depends only upon the Force of the Imagination, were
the Grounds of her liking the Poem, and afterwards of her Recommending
it to the Queen. I have likewise had the satisfaction to hear, that Her
Majesty has Graciously been pleased to peruse the Manuscript of this
Opera, and given it Her Royal Approbation. Poets, who subsist not but
on the Favour of Sovereign Princes, and of great Persons, may have
leave to be a little vain, and boast of their Patronage, who encourage the
Genius that animates them. And therefore I will again presume to ghess,
that Her Majesty was not displeas'd to find in this Poem the Praises of

Her Native Country; and the Heroick Actions of so famous a Predecessor in the Government of *Great Britain*, as King *Arthur*.

All this, My Lord, I must confess, looks with a kind of Insinuation, that I Present you with somewhat not unworthy of your Protection: But I may easily mistake the Favour of Her Majesty for Her Judgment: I think I cannot be deceiv'd in thus addressing to your Lordship, whom I have had the Honour to know, at that distance which becomes me, for so many Years. 'Tis true, that formerly I have shadow'd some part of your Virtues, under another Name; but the Character, though short and imperfect, was so true, that it broke through the Fable, and was discover'd by its Native Light. What I pretend by this Dedication, is an Honour which I do my self to Posterity, by acquainting them that I have been conversant with the first Persons of the Age in which I liv'd; and thereby perpetuate my Prose, when my Verses may possibly be forgotten, or obscur'd by the Fame of Future Poets. Which Ambition, amongst my other Faults and Imperfections, be pleased to pardon, in

MY LORD,

Your Lordship's most Obedient Servant,

John Dryden.[16]

Roger North has left the only eyewitness account of *King Arthur* on the stage.

I remember in Purcell's excellent opera of *King Arthur*, when Mrs Butler, in the person of Cupid, was to call up Genius, she had the liberty to turne her face to the scean, and her back to the theater. She was in no concerne for her face, but sang a *recitativo* of calling towards the place where Genius was to rise, and performed it admirably, even beyond any thing I ever heard upon the English stage.[17]

> What the performance was actually like we can only speculate, but North's comments elsewhere suggest that it would not meet modern performing standards.

But come into the theater or musick-meeting, and you shall have a woman sing like a mouse in a cheese, scarce to be heard, and for the most part her teeth shutt. And a consort of voices is scarce attempted: if one sings a plain part well, the rest by out-of-tune, or some other defect, spoyl all . . . What a fulsome thing it is to see a performer upon a stage not know when to begin, but the *basso continuo* must stay or skip for them,

which by the way they are not very good at: and then a flute must be at
the lasses ear to give her the tone, and that often thro' the whole air, or
else she would fall a semitone and sing on as assuredly as if she were in
no fault . . . Weoman are fearfull of the distortion of the face, which is
their *sanctum sanctorum*, therefore check the sound.[18]

> Sadly, the scenes, including the compelling Frost Scene, were
> unremarked by contemporaries, though the poet Thomas Gray
> (1716–71) was a witness to the 1735 revival. His letter of 3
> January 1736 to the littérateur Horace Walpole (1717–97),
> his friend at Eton and King's College, Cambridge, gives us
> some idea of the splendour of this scene when elaborately
> staged.

I went to King Arthur last night, which is exceeding fine; they have a
new man to [suppl]y Delane's place, one Johnson, with ye finest person
& face in the world to all appearance; but as awkward, as a Button-maker;
in short, if he knew how to manage his Beauties to advantage, I should
not wonder, if all the Woman run mad for him: the inchanted part of
the play, is not Machinery, but actual magick: the second scene is a
British temple enough to make one go back a thousand years, & really
be in ancient Britain: the Songs are all Church-musick, & in every one
of y[e] Chorus's M[rs] Chambers sung y[e] chief part, accompanied with

Roarings, Squawlings & Squeakations dire

M[rs] Giffard is by way of Emmeline, & should be blind, but, heaven
knows! I would not wish to see better than she does, & seems to do; for
when Philidel restores her to sight, her eyes are not all better than before;
she is led in at first, by a Creature, y[t] was more like a Devil by half, than
Grimbald himself; she took herself for Madame la Confidente, but every
body else took her to be in the Circumstances of Damnation: when Emmeline comes to her sight, she beholds this M[rs] Matilda first, & cries out

Are Women all like thee? Such glorious Creatures!

which set the people into such a laugh, as lasted the whole Act: the Frost
Scene is excessive fine; the first Scene of it is only a Cascade, that seems
frozen; with the Genius of Winter asleep & wrapt in furs, who upon the
approach of Cupid, after much quivering, & shaking sings the finest song
in the Play: just after, the Scene opens, & shows a view of arched rocks
covered with Ice and Snow to y[e] end of y[e] Stage; between the arches are

upon pedestals of Snow eight Images of old men & women, that seem frozen into Statues, with Icicles hanging about them & almost hid in frost, & from ye end come Singers, viz: Mrs Chambers, &c: & Dancers all rubbing their hands & chattering with cold with fur gowns & worsted gloves in abundance; there are several more Beautiful Scenes; but rather than describe 'em, I ought to beg pardon for interrupting your happiness so long.[19]

> A witness to an even later revival – the Cambridge production of 1928 – was the English novelist Sylvia Townsend Warner (1893–1978). Also a musicologist, she was one of the editors of *Tudor Church Music* (1923–9), and researched music of the fifteenth and sixteenth centuries. Cyril Rootham (1875–1938) was lecturer in music and organist of St John's College, while Edward Dent (1876–1957), the moving spirit behind the performance, was Professor of Music in the university from 1926 until 1941. Warner recorded the following memorable description of the evening.

To Cambridge, leaving my William behind at the Raymonds. Dined in Corpus with an air-marshal whose name I can't remember and then on to *King Arthur* by the Cambridge Operatic Society. Dryden simply could not go wrong when he wrote for the stage. There is no corner of the cheek his tongue was unacquainted with – the scene where Emmeline recovers her sight is almost Barrie-ish; yet over the whole is the nobility of a Godlike and rational technique. The music is neither Godlike nor rational – perhaps only Gluck's is: but O Lord how lovely and how English it is, English in its inadequacies, for Purcell's small-talk is all about the weather, and in its excellencies, its extraordinary poetry and eccentricity, queerness, authenticity of imagination . . .

At the end a speech from Rootham, involving a compliment to Dent. Dent retaliated from the house, and for one happy moment they both spoke at once, with the utmost civility and loathing in their tones. Young men in plus-fours and pull-overs walked onto the allegorical scene offering wreaths and brown paper parcels to the cast, and to Rootham a bowl of tulips, an unsuccessful bribe to make him leave off talking.[20]

THE FAIRY-QUEEN

The last dramatic opera to be completed by Purcell was *The Fairy-Queen*. As with *Dioclesian*, he returned to an old play, this time adapting Shakespeare's *Midsummer Night's Dream*. Although the author of the text remains anonymous, it is highly likely that Purcell had a hand in it. The first performance took place in 1692, and there was a revival in 1693; the first the public learned of it was in an announcement in Motteux's *Gentleman's Journal*.

Now I speak of Music I must tell you that we shall have speedily a New Opera, wherein something very surprising is promised us; Mr. *Purcel* who joyns to the Delicacy and Beauty of the *Italian* way, the Graces and Gayety of the *French*, composes the Music, as he hath done for the *Prophetess* [or *The History of Dioclesian*], and the last Opera called King *Arthur*, which hath been plaid several times the last Month. Other Nations bestow the name of Opera only on such Plays whereof every word is sung. But experience hath taught us that our English genius will not relish that perpetual Singing. I dare not accuse the Language for being over-charged with Consonants, which may take off the beauties of the Recitative part, tho' in several other Countries I have seen their *Opera's* still Crowded every time, tho long and almost all Recitative.[21]

Whereas Motteux simply says that experience had shown the English did not like all-sung opera, the author of the preface to the libretto uses a slightly different argument to justify the form of the opera: he claims, that speaking is 'music' anyway. He also includes a manifesto on funding national opera and on the economic benefits the arts bring to London, the sentiments of which have a familiar ring about them.

THE
PREFACE

'TIS *known to all who have been any considerable time in* Italy, *or* France, *how* Opera's *are esteem'd among 'em. That* France *borrow'd what she has from* Italy, *is evident from the* Andromede *and* Toison D'or, *of Monsieur* Corneille, *which are the first in the kind they ever had, on their publick Theaters; they being not perfect* Opera's, *but Tragedies, with Singing, Dan-*

1 The Restoration:
Charles and his Courtiers
on Horseguards Parade.
Walks such as this one in
front of the Palace of
Whitehall played an
important part in the
accessibility of the
monarchy.

2 Samuel Pepys, the
diarist, administrator and
music lover who chronicled
many of the events of the
Restoration including the
Plague and the Fire.

3 The Great Fire. A view from below London Bridge (left) showing the silhouettes of old St. Paul's Cathedral and a number of City churches, and the Tower of London (right). In the foreground can be seen the haphazard attempts by the populace to save their property which undoubtedly resulted in the 'good goods' observed by Pepys floating in the Thames.

Johannis Playford Effigies

4 John Playford. The Playfords – father John and son Henry – dominated the English publishing scene throughout Purcell's lifetime. The death of John Playford in 1686 inspired Purcell's 'Gentle Shepherd's, that you know', a setting of Nahum Tate's 'A pastoral elegy on the death of John Playford'.

5 John Evelyn. Another Restoration diarist, Evelyn also knew Pepys with whom he dined at the end of the century, hearing 'severall compositions of the last Mr. Purs esteemed the best composer of any Englishman hitherto'.

ohra Behn. The adventuress and first woman playwright, Behn heard 'Mr. P' sing
time during the early 1680s.

nry Purcell's Fantasia. The fantasia in 4 parts in g minor, z 735 dated 'June y^e
680', other fantasias quickly following on 11, 14, 19, 22, 23 and 30 June.

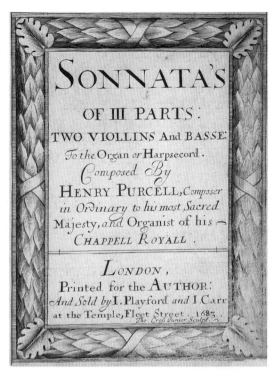

8 'Sonnata's of III Parts'. The title page of Purcell's 1683 volume containing works considered by the composer to be in the Italian style, but according to Roger North were 'colg'd with the English vein'.

10 *Opposite* James II and his Family. James and his first wife Anne Hyde, with the two princesses who successively became Queens Mary and Anne.

9 Ceremonial London. Painted around 1683, the Lord Mayor's water procession – an integral of the Lord Mayor's Pageant – moves past a backdrop of Westminster o its way to London.

Judge Jeffreys. Known as the 'Hanging Judge', Jeffreys was the adjudicator in Battle of the Organs' at the Temple Church; Purcell played the winning Smith n.

The Seven Bishops. The Bishops who defied the edict of James II, were tried released, and were the subject of Purcell's catch 'True Englishmen drink a good th to the mitre', z 284.

13 The Reception of William III. A stylized Dutch engraving showing the entry into the City of London by William of Orange.

14 The preface to *Dioclesian*. Purcell's signature in John Dryden hand was appended to the preface to the score of the opera, a text which declared that English music was 'yet but in its Nonage, a forward Child, which gives hope of what may be hereafter'.

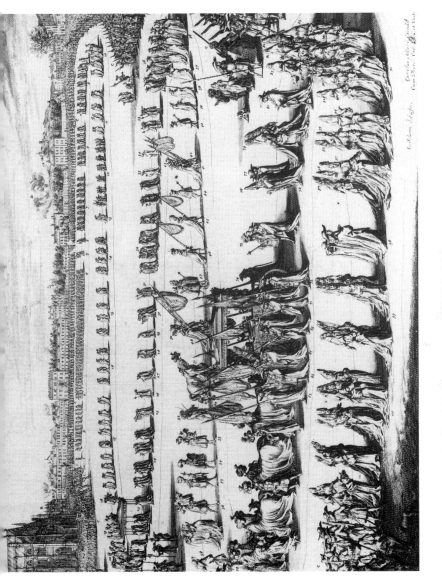

Queen Mary's Funeral. The funeral procession (with Her Majesty depicted lying up in the bier with her frontal on) moves through Westminster towards the Hawksmoor façade of the Abbey.

16 A Collection of Ayres
Compos'd for the Theatr[e]
A still life by Edward
Collier, with a composite
copy of Purcell's 1697
volume in pride of place;
the frontispiece is, in fac[t]
that from the 1697 sonata[s]
of 4 parts.

17 Lady Elizabeth
Howard's tablet to Purce[ll]
'Here Lyes Henry Purce[ll]
. . .'; the tablet was paid f[or]
by Lady Elizabeth
Howard, one of Purcell's
pupils and the dedicatee [of]
the first book of *Orpheus
Britannicus*.

cing, and Machines interwoven with 'em, after the manner of an Opera. *They give 'em a tast first, to try their Palats, and they might the better Judge whether in time they would be able to digest an entire* Opera. *And Cardinal* Richelieu *(that great Encourager of Arts and Learning) introduced 'em first at his own Expence, as I have been informed amongst' em.*

What encouragement Seignior Baptist Luly *had from the present King of* France, *is well known; they being first set out at his own Expence; and all the Ornaments given by the King, for the Entertainment of the People. In* Italy, *especially at* Venice, *where* Opera's *have the greatest Reputation, and where they have 'em every Carnival, the Noble* Venetians *set 'em out at their own cost. And what a Confluence of People the fame of 'em draw from all parts of* Italy *to the great profit of that city, is well known to every one who has spent a Carnival there. And many of the* English *Gentry are sensible what advantage* Paris *receives, by the great number of Strangers which frequent the* Opera's *three days in a Week, throughout the Year. If therefore an* Opera *were established here, by the Favour of the Nobility and Gentry of* England; *I may modestly conclude it would be some advantage to* London, *considering what a Sum we must Yearly lay out among Tradesmen for the fitting out so great a work.*

That Sir William Davenant's *Siege of* Rhodes *was the first* Opera *we ever had in* England, *no Man can deny; and is indeed a perfect* Opera: *there being this difference only between an* Opera *and a Tragedy; that the one is a Story sung with proper Action, the other spoken. And he must be a very ignorant Player, who knows not there is a Musical Cadence in speaking; and that a Man may as well speak out of Tune, as sing out of Tune. And though few are so nice as to examine this, yet all are pleas'd when they hear it justly perform'd. 'Tis true, the Siege of* Rhodes *wanted the Ornament of Machines, which they value themselves so much upon in* Italy. *And the Dancing which they have in such perfection in* France. *That he design'd this, if his first attempt met with the Encouragement it deserv'd, will appear from these Lines in his Prologue.*

> But many Travellers here, as Judges, come
> From *Paris, Florence, Venice,* and from *Rome.*
> Who will describe, when any Scene we draw,
> By each of ours, all that they ever saw.
> Those praising for extensive breadth and height,
> And inward distance to deceive the sight.——

And a little after——

Ah Mony, Mony! if the Wits would dress
With Ornaments the present face of Peace:
And to our Poet half that Treasure spare,
Which Faction gets from Fools to nourish War.
Then his contracted Scenes should wider be,
And move by greater Engines; till you see
(While you securely sit) fierce Armies meet,
And raging Seas disperse a fighting Fleet.

That a few private Persons should venture on so expensive a Work as an Opera, *when none but Princes, or States exhibit 'em abroad, I hope is no Dishonour to our Nation: And I dare affirm, if we had half the Encouragement in* England, *that they have in other Countries, you might in a short time have as good Dancers in* England *as they have in* France, *though I despair of ever having as good Voices among us, as they have in* Italy. *These are the two great things which Travellers say we are most deficient in. If this happens to please, we cannot reasonably propose to our selves any great advantage, considering the mighty Charge in setting it out, and the extraordinary expence that attends it every day 'tis represented. If it deserves their Favour? if they are satisfied we venture boldly, doing all we can to please 'em? We hope the* English *are too generous not to encourage so great an undertaking.*[22]

There were many surprising things in *The Fairy-Queen*, especially the spectacular stage directions. Even if the realization of such descriptions was less glamorous than the libretto suggests, the result must still have been impressive. In Act IV, for example:

The Scene changes to a Garden of Fountains. A Sonata plays while the Sun rises, it appears red through the Mist, as it ascends it dissipates the Vapours, and is seen in its full Lustre; then the Scene is perfectly discovered, the Fountains enrich'd with gilding, and adorn'd with Statues: The view is terminated by a Walk of Cypress Trees which lead to a delightful Bower. Before the Trees stand rows of Marble Columns, which support many Walks which rise by Stairs to the top of the House; the Stairs are adorn'd with Figures on Pedestals, and Rails; and Balasters on each side of 'em. Near the top, vast Quantities of Water break out of the Hills, and fall in mighty Cascade's to the bottom of the Scene, to feed the Fountains which are on each side. In the middle of the Stage is a very large Fountain, where the Water rises about twelve foot. [23]

> When the opera was staged, Motteux gives us the nearest
> thing to a contemporary review.

The OPERA of which I have spoken to you in my former [journal], hath at last appear'd, and continues to be represented daily; it is call'd, *The Fairy Queen*. The *Drama* is originally *Shakespears*, the *Music* and *Decorations* are extraordinary. I have heard the Dances commended, and without doubt the whole is entertaining. [24]

> That *The Fairy-Queen* also contained some unusual dramatic
> ideas is the subject of another passage by Roger North, who,
> while instructing the practitioner never to cease the basso
> continuo 'one moment', remembers – perhaps not quite accu-
> rately – something that impressed him in Purcell's score.

But yet, to shew how for representation or humour, every thing, even (seeming) absurditys may be made use of, there is a passage in [*The Fairy-Queen*] where in the midst of a full chorus, a rurall deity enters, and with a loud bass voice, sings, Peace. And then all the musique stopt all at once, and after a time the musick being resumed he sang, Silence, and was obeyed, a majesty in musick I have not observed in any I ever met with and even that silence kept the time. [25]

> Despite the popularity of *The Fairy-Queen*, the company seems
> to have mislaid the score fairly soon after the 1693 perform-
> ances, for we find in the *Flying Post* some years later:

The Score of Musick for the Fairy Queen, set by the late Mr Henry Pnrcel, and belonging to the Patentees of the Theatre-Royal in Covent-Garden, London, being lost upon his Death: Whoever shall bring the said Score, or a true Copy thereof, first to Mr. Zachary Baggs, Treasurer of the said Theatre, shall have twenty Guinea's for the same. [26]

> After Purcell's death many of his orchestral movements for
> the theatre appeared in *A Collection of Ayres Composed for the
> Theatre*, whose dedication read:

To His GRACE
CHARLES
Duke of Somerset,

Marquess and Earl of *HERTFORD*,
Viscount Beauchamp of *HATCHE*,
Baron *Seymour* of *TROWBRIDGE*,
Chancellor of the University of *CAMBRIDGE*,
Lord High Steward of *CHICHESTER*,
And *Knight* of the most Noble Order of the *GARTER*.

May it please Your Grace,
THE Favourable Reception which the following Compositions have found in the Theatre, *has given me some Hopes that they will meet with a suitable Encouragement from the Press: and as I am sensible that the Success of all Performances in this kind, as well as others, depends, not only upon their intrinsick Worth, but upon the Patronage of Illustrious and Judicious Persons, whose establish'd Reputation does often impute a Value to the Work they vouchsafe to Encourage; so in all that Number I could not find any One who has a better Title either to that Character, or to these Pieces, which, though to my great Misfortune, they are become Fatherless, yet I cannot fear they will be Friendless, whilst they are under the happy Influence of Your Grace's Protection.*

'Tis certain, that Duty as well as Interest, leads me to so Worthy a Choice, Your Grace having been pleas'd some time since to accept from my dear Husband, the Dedication of the Musick in Dioclesian, *part of which is contain'd, with some other Compositions of his, in these sheets; so that the Inscription of the whole Collection is justly due to Your Grace, whose Generous Encouragement of his Performances, as it has formerly laid the greatest Obligations upon his Person, so it will now continue them to his Posterity, and at the same time do the highest Honour to his Memory, which I promise my self from Your Grace's celebrated Goodness, will in some measure be as acceptable to Your Grace, as it is dear to*

Your Grace's most Oblig'd
and most Obediant Servant
FRANCES PURCELL.[27]

OPERA IN ENGLAND ASSESSED

Although Purcell and, after his death, composers such as
John Eccles and Jeremiah Clarke had considerable success in
producing dramatic operas, the genre never found a secure
place in the repertoire for a range of reasons, both aesthetic
and political. English opera was finally swamped by Italian
imports and drew stern criticism from many. The Italian
opera debate was to be held on and off throughout the eighteenth century, but during the first decades it was still in its
infancy. The desire to have an established English opera but
in the Italian style comes over strongly in an article in the
Muses Mercury, While praising Purcell, it damns dramatic
opera.

Of the Opera's *and* Plays *now Preparing for the two*
Theatres, in Drury-Lane *and the* Hay-Market

THE many excellent Productions of that great Master, the late Mr.
Henry Purcell, particularly his Opera of the *Prophetess*, that of King
Arthur, the Musical Parts of *Oedipus* and *Bonduca*, are sufficient Proofs
that no Nation in the World, the *Italians* only excepted, have out-done
the *English* in Dramatick *Musick*: And it is to be question'd, whether the
Italians in themselves come so near Nature, as Mr *Purcell* did in the
Musick of those Opera's and Plays; and whether there is any thing, so
moving at least, on the *Roman* and *Venetian* Stages. Perhaps our *Taste*
was to blame if he fell short of the Best Masters in *Italy*, by his accommo-
dating his *Compositions* to the *Relish* of his Audiences, for who can doubt
but he who Set the Frost *Scene* in *King Arthur*, cou'd have done any thing
in the great Musick whenever he attempted it.

'Tis plain that the Taste of the Town is mended since his Time, and
the late Success of *Arsinoe*, Set by Mr. *Clayton* after the *Italian* manner,
shews that our Masters can excel in all the Parts of Harmony, and our
Audiences *relish* them, as well as the *Italians*, that even their *Recitativo's*
have been heard with Delight, and consequently understood, which 40
Years ago wou'd have been receiv'd with the Disdain that Art meets with
from the Ignorant.[28]

When he discussed the failure of composers to write effective
recitative, North was driven to citing Nicholas Lanier's dia-

logue *Hero and Leander*, written after his return to England
from Italy in 1628.

The basso continuo is underwrote, which I presume may not disturbe
what belongs to the song; the rest expresseth passion, hope, fear, and
despair, as strong as words and sounds can bear, and saving some pieces
of Mr. H. Purcell, wee have nothing of this kind in English at all
recommendable.[29]

> A writer who continued to work towards the development of
> a more critical approach to the stage was Charles Gildon
> (1665–1724). His many works included the 'improvement'
> of what was one of Shakespeare's most unpopular plays,
> *Measure for Measure*, by inserting in the action Purcell's *Dido
> and Aeneas* as a series of masques. His two most valuable
> studies were *The Complete Art of Poetry* (1718) and his *Life
> of Thomas Betterton* (1710), both of which contain passages
> on Purcell's operas. In considering the Italian operas being
> staged in London, Gildon wrote that they

touch the head by their Lightness, but never reach the Heart. But *Harry
Purcel* seem'd to have the Genius of *Greek* Musick; he touch'd the Soul;
he made his Way to the Heart, and by that Means, left a satisfaction in
the Pleasure, when past. He had the Art of Painting in Musick, which
Aristotle mentions of the *Greek* Musicians; witness his *Frost Scene*, where,
by the admirable Conjunction of Flats and Sharps, he makes you almost
shiver both with his Instrumental and Vocal Musick.[30]

> In his *Life of Thomas Betterton* Gildon reprinted a letter
> of 1678 to the Duke of Buckingham from the French
> writer and wit Charles de Saint Denis, Seigneur de
> Saint-Évremond (1610–1703), who discoursed
> unflatteringly on the merits of French and Italian opera,
> concluding that opera 'is a very ODD MEDLEY *of*
> POETRY *and* MUSIC, in which the Poet and Master
> of Music are equally on the Rack for one another, and
> take a great deal of Pains to compose a very Scurvy-
> Piece'. Gildon replied:

But this Author [Saint-Évremond] puts a great Stress on the *Taking* of
his Compositions, and the Miscarriage of those of others, when he had

before deny'd, that we knew any thing of the Matter. But if he allow[s] that, as a Test of the Excellence of his *Opera*, that will be much stronger for Mr. *Henry Purcel*, whose Music supported a Company of young raw Actors, against the best and most favour'd of that Time, and transported the Town for several Years together, as they do yet all true Lovers of Music. Let any Master compare *Twice ten hundred Deities*, the Music in the *Frost Scene*, several Parts of the *Indian Queen*, and twenty more Pieces of *Henry Purcel*, with all the *Arrieto's*, *Dacapo's*, *Recitativo's* of *Camilla*, *Pyrrhus*, *Clotilda*, &c. and then judge which excels. *Purcel* penetrates the Heart, makes the Blood dance through your Veins, and thrill with the agreeable Violence offer'd by his Heavenly Harmony; the *Arietto's* are pretty light Airs, which tickle the Ear, but reach no farther; *Purcel* moves the Passions as he pleases, nay, *Paints* in Sounds, and verifies all that is said of *Timotheus*. Music, as well as Verse, is subject to that Rule of *Horace*;

> *He that would have Spectators share his Grief,*
> *Must write not only well, but movingly.*

This was *Henry Purcel's* Talent; and *his* MUSIC, as known as it is, and as often repeated as it has been, has to this Day the very same Effect. But all the Airs of these *Opera's*, as they touch nothing but the Ear, so they vanish as soon, as that is try'd with the Repetition; that is, they live but a Year at most; so that *Purcel's* being compos'd to penetrate the Soul, and make the Blood thrill through the Veins, live for ever; but those foreign Whims, which have cost us above twenty thousand Pounds, are lost before the Castratos have spent the Money they brought them in.

But it has by this very Book been said, that our Taste is improv'd, much amended since the Time of *Henry Purcel*, and that we should not now relish any of his Things. To this I answer, that I find the best Judges of Music, those who are Masters of the Composition, as well as Performance, prefer what he has done to all the *Opera's* we have had, on our Stage at least. I would therefore fain know how our Taste is mended? Do the promiscuous Audience know more of the Art of Harmony and Music? No — not one in a thousand understands one single Note. How shall these therefore give the Preference of this new *Music*, to that of *Henry Purcel's*? The Masters must decide it, you reply perhaps — That indeed would bring it into a small Compass, to the Decision of a very few, and yet not to be determin'd; for the *English* Masters have still a

Veneration for *Purcel*; and the Foreign Masters have too visible an interest to be the Deciders. The only way is by the Rules of Art; for what goes beyond them is nothing but Extravagance, and no Beauty; and if the *Italians* sing out of Tune by way of Perfection, they must enjoy the Advantage, which all Men else in the World will condemn as no Harmony, and by Consequence can be no Beauty or Excellence in Music, the very Soul of which is *Harmony*.[31]

> The versatile writer and adventurer Daniel Defoe (1660–1731) spent much of his time in pamphleteering and political manoeuvring; in 1715 the two activities came together in his pamphlet *Appeal to Honour and Justice*, which attempts to justify his career as a double agent. Around 1719 he began to produce fiction, his best-known pieces being *Robinson Crusoe* and *Moll Flanders*. In 1728 he wrote *Augusta Triumphans, or the Way to make London the most Flourishing City in the Universe*, which included the following passage on the importance of a national opera.

Would it not be a glorious thing to have an *Opera* of our own, in our own most noble Tongue, in which the Composer, Singers, and Orchestre, should be of our own Growth? Not that we ought to disclaim all Obligations to *Italy*, the Mother of Musick, the Nurse of *Corelli*, *Handel*, *Bononcini*, and *Geminiani*; but then we ought not to be so stupidly partial, to imagine our Selves too Brutal a part of Mankind, to make any Progress in the Science . . . We have already had a *Purcel*, and no doubt, there are now many latent Genius's, who only lack proper Instruction, Application, and ENCOURAGEMENT, to become great Ornaments of the Science, and make *England* emulate even *Rome* it self.[32]

> One of the most eloquent assessments of Purcell's operas, and one which also considers the audience's expectations, was made in the twentieth century by the English organist Sir George Dyson (1883–1964). Dyson composed numerous works for the church and concert hall, and was director of the Royal College of Music from 1937 until 1952. His most important book was *The New Music*, which examined the techniques of 'modern' composition, but in his more wide-ranging volume, *The Progress of Music*, he gives what might be described as the received twentieth-century view of Purcell's operas.

The works which Purcell wrote for the public stage were operas only by some stretching of the term. The public wanted engaging songs and lively dances, and Purcell could provide these with unfailing freshness and beauty. It also wanted exotic scenery, strange costume, and new mechanical ingenuities. And no one could hit off an odd situation in music better than Purcell could. Of consistent plot, reasoned character-drawing, or indeed any of the dramatic conditions of credibility, there was no need, for these things were not in demand. What was desired was a variety entertainment, and the disjointed operas of Purcell supplied it. There are isolated scenes of great musical beauty, with many a moment of inspired resource. There are delightful songs and duets, grave and gay, on which Purcell lavished his incomparable gifts of melody and wordpainting, and there are scores of preludes, interludes, and dances which are perennially fragrant. These gems remain, but they are immersed in a mass of inconsequent incidents, and they have never recovered from this initial chaos. Purcell's public had no wish for consistent unfolding of an extended and unified design. They wanted a dramatic and musical medley. They got what they wanted, and the first and most golden chance of native opera vanished in the process. If Purcell had had the opportunities of some of his contemporaries in Italy and France, every opera-house in Europe would have clamoured for his music. He might in due time have been imported back into England, and given the status rarely bestowed on an English-born.[33]

VII

'O mourn, ye sacred Muses, mourn'

How Purcell met his end is obscure. Hawkins repeats the
probably apocryphal story that

his death was occasioned by a cold which he caught in the night, waiting
for admittance into his own house. It is said that he used to keep late
hours, and that his wife had given orders to his servants not to let him
in after midnight: unfortunately he came home heated with wine from
the tavern at an hour later than that prescribed him, and through the
inclemency of the air contracted a disorder of which he died.[1]

This bespeaks a lack of sympathy which belies Frances Purcell's true nature if Hawkins's writing elsewhere is to be
believed:

when the report of Stradella's assassination reached the ears of Purcell,
and he was informed jealousy was the motive to it, he lamented his fate
exceedingly; and, in regard of his great merit as a musician, said he could
have forgiven him any injury in that kind; which, adds the relator, 'those
who remember how lovingly Mr. Purcell lived with his wife, or rather
what a loving wife she proved to him, may understand without farther
explication.'[2]

Whatever the truth of the matter, by 21 November 1695 he
was so ill that three friends were called to witness his will.

In the name of God Amen. I, Henry Purcell, of the City of Westminster,
gentleman, being dangerously ill as to the constitution of my body, but
in good and perfect mind and memory (thanks be to God) do by these
present publish and declare this to be my last will and testament. And I
do hereby bequeath unto my loving wife, Frances Purcell, all my estate
both real and personal of what nature and kind soever, to her and to her
assigns for ever. And I do hereby constitute and appoint my said loving
wife my sole executrix of this my last Will and Testament, revoking all
former Will or Wills, witness my hand and seal this twenty-first day of

November, Annoque Domini one thousand six hundred ninety five. And
in the seventh year of the reign of King William the Third &c. H.
Purcell.

Signed, sealed published, and declared by the said Henry Purcell in
the presence of William Esles, John Chapelin, J. B. Peters.[3]

> The *Flying Post* reported:

Mr. *Henry Pursel*, one of the most Celebrated *Masters* of the Science of
Musick in the Kingdom, and scarce Inferiour to any in Europe, dying
on Thursday last; the Dean of Westminster knowing the great worth of
the deceased, forthwith summoned a Chapter, and unanimously resolved
that he shall be interred in the Abbey, with all the Funeral Solemnity
they are capable to perform for him, granting his Widow the choice of
the ground to Reposite his Corps free from any charge, who has appointed
it at the foot of the Organs, and this Evening he will be Interred, the
whole Chapter assisting with their vestments; together with all the Lovers
of that Noble Science, with the united Choyres of that and the Chappel
Royal, when the Dirges composed by the Deceased for her late Majesty
of Ever Blessed Memory, will be Played by Trumpets and other
Musick; And his place of Organist is disposed to that great Master, Dr.
Blow.[4]

> There followed a bleak announcement in the *Post Boy*.

London, Novemb. *28th*. Dr. *Purcel* was Interred at *Westminster* on *Tuesday*
night in a magnificent manner. He is much lamented, being a very great
Master of Musick.[5]

> His patroness and the dedicatee of the first book of *Orpheus*
> *Britannicus*, Lady Annabella Howard, arranged for the tablet
> which was placed in a pillar in Westminster Abbey.

Here lyes
HENRY PURCELL, Esq.;
Who left this Life
And is gone to that Blessed Place,
Where only his Harmony
can be exceeded
Obiit 21mo. die Novembrs,
Anno Ætatis suæ 37mo,

Annoq Domini 1695.[6]

Since she was the wife of John Dryden, it is possible that, as
Walter Scott suggested, Dryden was responsible for the word-
ing of her tablet.

FRANCES PURCELL
(?–1706)

Purcell's wife had great cause to mourn. Not only had she
been widowed, but she was left without an income. The depth
of feeling that comes through the dedications to the first book
of *Orpheus Britannicus* and the 1697 sonatas is unlike the
somewhat vacuous sentiments usually found in this type of
inscription. Frances's dedicatee of the 1697 sonatas was a
former pupil of Purcell, Lady Rhoda Cavendish. Despite her
aristocratic connections, little is known of Rhoda Cavendish,
née Cartwright, of Aynhoe. She married Lord Henry Cavendish, MP for Derby, in 1696; he died of the palsy in 1700,
leaving her with one daughter, Mary, with whom she appears
to have quarrelled bitterly. She studied with Purcell during
the early 1690s, with some success, according to the dedication.

To the Right Honourable Lady Rhoda Cavendish:

MADAM,

THE following Collection having already found many Friends among
the Judicious part of Mankind, I was desirous that it might not want the
Patronage of our Sex, for whose Honour, as well as for the Credit of this
Work, I have presum'd to place Your Ladyship's Name before these
Sheets. And certainly, Madam, my Ambition will be justify'd by all
that have the Happiness of knowing Your Excellent Judgment, and the
wonderfull Progress You have made (beyond most of either Sex) in all
Ingenuous Accomplishments, and particularly in this of Musick, for
which you have often been Admir'd by the dear Author of these Compositions; whose Skill in this Science is best recommended to the World by
telling it, that He had the Honour to be Your Master: upon whose
Account, as well as on that of many Personal Obligations, I am prompted

by Gratitude no less than Ambition to acknowledge my self in the most
Publick manner,

> Your Ladyship's most Oblig'd
> and most Obediant Servant,
>
> FRANCES PURCELL[7]

Orpheus Britannicus was dedicated to Lady Howard, probably
in recognition of her payment for the tablet over Purcell's
tomb. It did not appear immediately, the delays being
explained by Henry Playford in a note at the end of An
Introduction to the Skill of Musick.

By reason of the small Encouragement, and for the more compleat Printing of that Excellent Master Mr. H. Purcell's Vocal and Instrumental
Musick in all their Parts, a longer Time is given to Subscribers, hoping
by Trinity-Term next to meet with greater Encouragement, so that Subscriptions will be taken till then, and the Book deliver'd at the end of that
Term: Proposals are to be had at H. Playford's Shop; where will be
speedily publish'd, a Catalogue of all the Musick Books sold at the same
place, in which will be several Italian Musick-Books, and some newly
come over.[8]

The collection, which consisted of 'all the choicest songs for
one, two and three voices . . . together with such symphonies
for violins or flutes as were design'd for any of 'em', was a
posthumous anthology of monumental proportions that contained many of Purcell's best-loved songs.

> To the Honourable,
> The Lady HOWARD.

MADAM,
Were it in the power of Musick to abate those strong Impressions of
Grief which have continued upon me ever since the Loss of my dear
lamented Husband, there are few (I believe) who are furnished with
larger or better supplies of Comfort from this Science, than he has left
me in his own Compositions, and in the Satisfaction I find, that they are
not more valued by me (who must own my self fond to a Partiality of all
that was his) than by those who are no less Judges than Patrons of his
Performances. I find, Madam, I have already said enough to justifie the

Presumption of this Application to Your Ladiship, who have added both these Characters to the many excellent Qualities, which make You the Admiration of all that know You. Your Ladiship's extraordinary skill in Musick, beyond most of either Sex, and Your great Goodness to that dear Person, whom You have sometimes been pleased to honour with the Title of Your Master, makes it hard for me to judge whether he contributed more to the vast Improvements You have made in that Science, or Your Ladiship to the Reputation he gain'd in the Profession of it: For I have often heard him say, That as several of his best Compositions were originally design'd for Your Ladiship's Entertainment, so the Pains he bestowed in fitting them for Your Ear, were abundantly rewarded by the Satisfaction he has received from Your Approbation, and admirable Performance of them, which has best recommended both them and their Author to all that have had the happiness of hearing them from Your Ladiship.

Another great advantage, to which my Husband has often imputed the success of his Labors, and which may best plead for Your Ladiship's favourable Acceptance of this Collection, has been the great Justness both of Thought and Numbers which he found in the Poetry of our most refin'd Writers, and among them, of that Honourable Gentleman, who has the dearest and most deserved Relation to your Self, and whose Excellent Compositions were the Subject of his last and best Performance in Musick.

Thus, Madam, Your Ladiship has ever way the justest Title to the Patronage of this Book, the Publication of which, under the auspicious Influence of Your Name, is the best (I had almost said the only) means I have left of Testifying to the World, my desire to pay the last Honours to its dear Author, Your Ladyship having generously prevented my intended Performance of the Duty I owe to his Ashes, by erecting a fair Monument over them, and gracing it with an Inscription which may perpetuate both the Marble and his Memory. Your Generosity, which was too large to be confin'd either to his Life or his Person, has also extended it self to his Posterity, on whom Your Ladiship has been pleas'd to entail Your Favours, which must, with all Gratitude, be acknowledg'd as the most valuable part of their Inheritance, both by them, and

YOUR LADISHIP'S

Most oblig'd, and most Humble Servant,

Fr. Purcell.[9]

The publisher of *Orpheus Britannicus*, Henry Playford, included the following exhortation.

THE
Bookseller to the Reader.

Whereas this Excellent Collection was design'd to have been Publish'd some considerable Time before now, the Reason of its delay, was to have it as compleat as possibly it could be made, both in regard to the Memory of that great Master, and the Satisfaction of all that buy it. And to make amends to those Gentlemen and Ladies who subscrib'd early to this Work, they will here find an Addition of above Thirty Songs more than were at first propos'd which (considering the extraordinary charge of Paper, &c at this time) is an additional Expence to me, tho' I hope the Completness of the Work will recompence my Care and Trouble. The Author's extraordinary Talent in all sorts of Musick is sufficiently known, but he was especially admir'd for the Vocal, *having a peculiar Genius to express the Energy of* English *Words, whereby he mov'd the Passions of all his Auditors. And I question not, but the Purchaser will be very pleas'd in the Choice of this Collection, which will be a great Satisfaction to*

Your Humble Servant,

Hen. Playford.[10]

The second book of *Orpheus Britannicus* was dedicated to Charles Halifax, a choice that was probably entirely Playford's.

To the Right Honourable
Charles, Lord Hallifax,
Auditor of His Majesties Exchequer, *&c.*

MY LORD,

I *Shou'd be unjust to the Memory of the admired* Purcell, *and set too Small a Value on His Works, shou'd I put them under any Patronage but Your own. For Your* Lordship *has a Double Title to these Papers, both as You are the best Judge, as well as the Greatest Encourager of* Poesy *and* Musick. *'Tis but fit this Great Master of the Age, that has stood the Test of Your Judgment, should Claim Your Protection: Since no Greater Character can be given of any Composition, than that it has pleas'd so Exquisite a Taste as Your* Lordship's.

But I am not so vain, as to attempt a Panegyrick on Your Lordship, *nor to Expatiate on the several Excellencies of this Celebrated Author: These are subjects for the Sublimest Pens, and are already transmitted to Posterity.*

But my design here, is to pay my Gratitude to Your Lordship, *for the many Favours I have receiv'd; In a Present whose own Worth, is its Apology, and whose Native Graces will render it Acceptable. And to add, if possible to the Fame of* Purcell, *and Endear him more to the World: Which can be only done, by prefixing the Name of* Mountague *to His Works.*

My Lord,
I am Your Lordships most Humble and Obliged Servant.
HENRY PLAYFORD[11]

This time Playford's note to the reader was almost solely concerned with the commercial aspects of the publication and the justification of his own activities as a publisher.

The Bookseller to the
READER.

The late Publication of these Excellent Performances in *Musick*, is sufficiently aton'd for, by the Care that has been taken in the Collection of 'em; and I cannot but think I have made amends enough to the Purchaser in the Choice of 'em. The great Charge I have been at; the Diligence I have made use of to obtain the Assistance of Friends, and the Dearness of Paper in which these Admirable Composers are transmitted to the Publick, are sufficient Excuses: And I shall insist upon that Subject no farther, Than that as I have always been employed in promoting the encrease of things of this Nature, and contributed to the utmost towards their Encouragement, so I shall still make it my Endeavours to go on with so Laudable an Undertaking. I might indeed make my Compliments in relation to the greatness of my Expenses in being Beneficial to the Publick, and Expose some People that build upon my Foundation; but as I desire the Readers Candour, it's my Business to make use of it in Respect to others, only I shall take notice, I have more than enough Discouragement to drop the pursute of Obliging my Country, since Foreigners meet with a reception that is inconsistent with the Interest of one, that has the Honour to be a Native. But let 'em Undersell me as long as they please, and Transplant their Foreign Musick into these

Climates, the Judicious will be of my side, when they make an Estimate of Mr *Purcell's* works, which are equal to those of the Best Masters of *Italy*, and conclude, that I, who have now made a compleat Collection of all his Choicest Performances, deserve a better Entertainment from the Hands of the Publick, than any Pretenders whatsoever.

H.P.[12]

> One of the features – though not an unusual one – of *Orpheus Britannicus* was the inclusion of a large number of poems in the front of the volume, lamenting the loss of the great composer. They came from a range of friends, scholars and collaborators, not all identifiable but all heartfelt. John Dryden's 'Ode on the Death of Mr Henry Purcell', set to music by John Blow, was probably the finest contribution.

An ODE
on the Death of Mr. Henry Purcell.
Written by *Mr*. Dryden.

Mark how the Lark and Linnet Sing,
With rival Notes
They strain their warbling Throats,
To welcome in the Spring.
But in the close of Night,
When *Philomel* begins her Heav'nly Lay,
They cease their mutual spight,
Drink in her Musick with Delight,
And list'ning and silent, and silent and list'ning,
   And list'ning and silent obey.

So ceas'd the rival Crew when *Purcell* came,
They Sung no more, or only Sung his Fame.
Struck dumb they all admir'd the God-like Man:
  The God-like Man,
  Alas! too soon retir'd,
  As He too late began.
We beg not Hell our *Orpheus* to restore:
  Had he been there,
  Their Sovereigns fear
  Had sent him back before.

The pow'r of Harmony too well they knew,
He long e're this had Tun'd their jarring Sphere,
      And left no Hell below.

The Heav'nly Quire, who heard his Notes from high,
Let down the Scale of Musick from the Sky:
      They handed him along,
And all the way He taught, and all the way they Sung.
      Ye Brethren of the *Lyre*, and tunefull Voice,
      Lament his lot, but at your own rejoyce.
      Now live secure and linger out your days,
      The Gods are pleas'd alone with *Purcell's* Layes,
      Nor know to mend their Choice.[13]

JOHN SHEFFIELD, EARL OF MULGRAVE, *LATER* DUKE OF BUCKINGHAM
(1648–1721)

Not included in *Orpheus Britannicus* was John Sheffield's 'Ode on the Death of Henry Purcell'. Its significance lay not in the quality of its verse, but the author's social position, his role as an arbiter of taste and his earlier dismissal of the possibility that England had produced a composer of any stature.

ODE *on the Death of* Henry Purcell,
Set to Musick.

Good Angels snatch'd him eagerly on high;
Joyful they flew, singing, and soaring thro' the Sky,
      Teaching his new fledg'd Soul to fly;
      While we, alas, lamenting lie.
    He went musing all along,
    Composing new their heav'nly Song.
A while his skillful Notes loud Hallelujah's drown'd;
But soon they ceas'd their own, to catch his pleasing Sound
      David himself improv'd the Harmony,
      David in sacred Story so renown'd
    No less for Musick, than for Poetry!

Genius sublime in either Art:
Crown'd with Applause surpassing all Desert!
A Man just after God's own Heart!
If human Cares are lawful to the Blest,
Already settled in eternal Rest;
Needs must he with that *Purcell* only might
Have liv'd to set what he vouchsaf'd to write.
For, sure, the noble Thirst of Fame
With the frail Body never dies;
But with the Soul ascends the Skies
From whence at first it came.
'Tis sure no little Proof we have
That part of us survives the Grave,
And in our Fame below still bears a Share:
Why is the Future else so much our Care,
Ev'n in our latest Moment of Despair?
And Death despis'd for Fame by all the wise and brave?
Oh, all ye blest harmonious Quire!
Who Pow'r Almighty only love, and only that admire!
Look down with Pity from your peaceful Bow'r
On this sad Isle perplex'd,
And ever, ever vex'd
With anxious Care of Trifles, Wealth, and Pow'r.
In our rough Minds due Reverence infuse
For sweet melodious Sounds, and each harmonious Muse.
Musick exalts Man's Nature, and inspires
High elevated Thoughts, or gentle, kind Desires.[14]

Another who regretted Purcell's death was the diarist John
Evelyn. On visiting Samuel Pepys in 1698, he listened to
the singing of the English countertenor John Pate (?–1704),
who had made his first appearance in Purcell's *Fairy-Queen*
in 1692. Later in his colourful life he was incarcerated in the
Bastille and condemned to death on the wheel for 'killing a
man'; fortunately for singing in England, nothing seems to
have come of this.

I dined at Mr. Pepyss, where I heard that rare Voice, Mr. *Pate*, who
was lately come from *Italy*, reputed the most excellent singer, ever

England had: he sang indeede many rare Italian Recitatives, &c: & severall compositions of the last Mr. Pursal, esteemed the best composer of any Englishman hitherto.[15]

GEORGE GRANVILLE, BARON LANSDOWNE
(1667–1735)

The dramatist and poet George Granville wrote a number of dramas and adaptations, and was the author of the dramatic opera *The British Enchanters* (performed in 1706). He went on to have a successful political career, to become an early patron of Pope and to be the author of some indifferent verse. His early epilogue to his adaptation of Shakespeare's *Merchant of Venice*, however, is a sharp comment on the theatrical difficulties which afflicted the London theatre around the time of Purcell's death. The poet and the priest in the first line are John Dryden and Jeremy Collier, and the performers in the last line are from the ranks of prize-fighters and rope-dancers. Purcell's 'Syren Song' is the masque he set for a revival of *Timon of Athens*.

> Each in his turn, the Poet and the Priest,
> Have view'd the Stage, but like false Prophets guess'd:
> The Man of Zeal in his Religious Rage
> Would silence Poets, and reduce the Stage.
> The Poet rashly, to get clear, retorts
> On Kings the Scandal, and bespatters Courts.
> Both err; for without mincing, to be plain,
> The Guilt is yours of every Odious Scene.
> The present time still gives the Stage its Mode,
> The Vices which you practice, we explode:
> We hold the Glass, and but reflect your Shame,
> Like Spartans, by exposing, to reclaim.
> The Scribler, pinch'd with Hunger, writes to Dine,
> And to your Genius must conform his Line;
> Not lewd by Choice, but meerly to submit;
> Would you encourage Sense, Sense would be writ.

Plain Beauties pleas'd your Sires an Age ago,
Without the Varnish and the Dawb of Show.
At vast Expence we labour to our Ruine,
And count your Favour with our own undoing.
A War of Profit mitigates the Evil,
But to be tax'd and beaten, is the Devil.
How was the Scene forlorn, and how despis'd,
When Tymon, *without Musick, moraliz'd?*
Shakespears *sublime in vain entic'd the Throng,*

Without the Charm of Purcel's *Syren Song.*
In the same Antique Loom these Scenes were wrought,
Embelish'd with good Morals and just Thought:
True Nature in her Noblest Light you see, ⎫
E're yet debauch'd by modern Gallantry,   ⎬
To triffling Jest, and fulsom Ribaldry.   ⎭
What Rust remains upon the shinning Mass
Antiquity may privilege to pass.
'Tis Shakespear's *Play, and if these Scenes miscarry,*
Let Gormon *take the Stage — or Lady Mary.*[16]

VIII

From beyond the grave

THOMAS BROWN

(1663–1704)

Perhaps the most amusing commentary on the Restoration musical scene is contained in Thomas Brown's *Letters from the Dead to the Living*, published in the early eighteenth century. As the title suggests, the fictional correspondence consists of epistles from a range of deceased worthies, together with replies from their recipients, those of interest here being Henry Purcell and John Blow respectively. From Purcell's praise of the new world around him and from Blow's trenchant criticism of that which his friend has left, an evocative picture of life in and around Westminster Abbey and the playhouses emerges. Thomas Brown, author of the famous response 'I do not love you Dr Fell', was, in the words of Arthur L. Hayward, 'one of the best of Grub Street's literary hacks – scholarly, witty, scurrilous and unscrupulous' and 'an excellent journalist with a sure instinct for a good "story" '.

From Henry Purcel *to Doctor* B—w.

Dear Friend,

TO tell you the truth, I sent you this Letter on purpose to undeceive you; I know that the upper World has a notion, that these Infernal shades are destitute of all Harmony, and delight in nothing but Jarring, Discord and Confusion; upon the word of a Musician, you are all mistaken, for I never came into a merrier Country, since I knew a Whimsy from a Fiddle-stick; every Body here Sings as Naturally as a Nightingale, and at least as sweet. Lovers sit perched upon Boughs by pairs, like murmuring Turtles in a rural Grove, and in Amorous Ditties sing forth their passionate Affections; all People on this side [of] the Adamantine Gates have their Organs perfect, and *I burn, I burn, I burn*, which some Persons have thought a critical Song upon Earth, is here Sung by every Scoundrel: The whole Infernal Territory is infested with such innumerable Crouds of Poets and Musicians, that a Man can't stir twice his length, but he shall Tread upon a New Ballad; and as for Musick, it's so plenty among us, that a Fellow shall be scraping upon a Fiddle at every Garrett-window, and anothor tinkling a Spinet, or a Virginal in every Chimney Corner; Flutes, Hoitboys, and Trumpets are so perpetually Tooting, that all the

Year round the whole Dominion is like a *Bartholemew-Fair*; and as for
Drums, you have a set of them under every Devils Window, Ratling and
Thumping like a Concert of His Majesty's Rat-tat-too's at an *English*
Wedding: We have such a glut of all sorts of performers, that our very
Ears are surfeited; and any Body may hire a Concert for a Day, large
enough to surround *Westminster-Abbey*, for the price of a Hundred of
Chestnuts; yet every Minstrel performs to admiration. Every Cobler here
that dispatches a Voluntary, whilst he's Waxing his Thred, shall out sing
Mr. *Ab—l*, and a Carpenter shall make better Musick up on an Empty
Cupboard strung with five Brass-wires, than *Bap—st* can upon the Harpsi-
chord; every Trumpet that attends a Bodkin Lottery sounds bettter than
Sh—re; and not a Porter here Plies at the corner of a Srreet, but with his
stubbed Fingers, can make a smooth Table outgrunt the Harmony of a
double Curtel. We have Catches too in admirable perfection: Fish-Women
sit and Sing them at Market, instead of Scolding as they do at *Billinsgate*;
Hymns and Anthems are as frequent among us as among you of the upper
World; For to every Church God Almighty has on Earth here, the Devil
has a Chappel. You are sensible I was a great Lover of Musick before I
departed my Temporal Life, but now I am so surfeited with incessant
sound, that I would rather chuse to be as deaf as an Adder, than be
plagu'd with the best *Ayre* that ever *Corella* made, or the finest *Sola* or
Sonetta that ever was Compos'd in *Italy*: For you must know the Laws of
this Country are such, that every Man, for his Sins in the other World,
shall here be punish'd with excess of that which he there esteem'd most
pleasant and delightful. Lovers that in your Region would Hang, or
Drown, or run thro' fire like a couple of Salamanders for one another's
Company, are here coupled together like the Twins *Castor* and *Pollux*,
pursuant to their own wishes upon Earth, and have all the Liberty they
can desire with one another, but must never be separated whilst Eternity
endures: This sort of confinement, tho' 'tis what they once coveted, makes
them so Sick of one another in a little time, that they cry out, O Damnable
Slavery! O Diabolical Matrimony! and are always drawing Two several
ways with all imaginable Hatred, endevouring to break their Fetters, and
pursue variety; thus every one is Wedded to what they like best, and yet
every person's desires terminates in their own Misery, which sufficiently
shews there is no other Justice to punish us for our follies, than the
Objects of our own loose Appetites and Inclinations; for that which we
are apt to covet most when we are in the upper World, generally, if

obtain'd, proves our greatest unhappiness; therefore, since experience would not teach us to bridle our Inclinations on the other side of the Grave, the Pleasures we pursued when we were Living, are after Death appointed to be our Punishments.

Doctor *Stag—s*, is greatly improved since he arriv'd in these Parts, and has more Crotchets flows thro' his Brains in one Minute, than he can digest into Musick in a whole Week; he had not been here a Month, but his Bandy-Legs stept into a very good Place, and his Business to Compose *Scotch* Tunes for *Lucifer's* Bag-piper. Honest *Tom Farmer* has taken such an Antipathy against Musick, upon hearing a *French* Barber Play *Bannister's* Ground in *Bemi*, upon a Jews-Trump, that he swears that the Hooping of a Tub, and Filing of a Saw, makes the sweetest Harmony in Christendom. *Robin Smith* is still as Love-mad as ever he was; hangs half a dozen Fiddles at his Girdle, as the Fellow does his Coneyskins and scrowers up and down Hell, crying a *Reevs*, a *Reevs*, as if the Devil was in him. Poor *Vol Redding* too is quite tired with his Lireway Fiddle, and has betaken himself to be a merry-Andrew to a *Dutch* Mountebank; and the Reason he gave for it was this, that he was got into a Country where he found Fools were more respected than Fidlers. Dancing-Masters are also as numerous in every Street, as Posts in *Cheapside*, there is no walking but we must stumble upon them; they are held here but in very slight Esteem, for the Gentry call them Leg-livers, and the Mob from their mighty Number, and their Nimbleness, call them the Devils Grasshoppers. Players run up and down muttering of old Speeches, like so many Madmen in their Sililoques; and if any Beau wants a Bridge to bear him over a dirty Channel, a Player lies down instead of a Plank, for him to walk over upon; the reason why they were doom'd to the piece of scandalous Servitude, was, because they were as Proud upon the Stage as the very Princes they represented; and as Humble in a Brandy-shop, as a Scold in a Ducking-stool; therefore were fit for nothing when they had done Playing but to be trampled upon. I have nothing further at present to impart to you, so begging you to excuse this trouble,

> *I rest*
> *Your Humble Servant*
> Henry Purcel.

Dr. B—'s *Answer to* Henry Purcel.

Dear Friend,

YOUR Letter was one of the greatest surprises to me, I ever met with; for after giving Credit to that fulsome piece of Flattery, stuck up by some of your Friends upon a Pillar behind the Organ which you once was Master of, I remain'd satisfied you were gone to that happy place where your own Harmony could only be exceeded, and had left orders with some of your Friends to put up that Epitaph only as a direction where your Acquaintance upon occasion might be sure to meet with you: but since you have favour'd me with a Letter from your own Hand, wherein you assure me 'twas your Fortune to travel a quite contrary Road, I will always be of the Opinion for the future, that when a Man takes a step in the dark, those that he leaves behind him can no more guess where he is gone, than I can tell what's become of the Saddle which *Balaam* Rid upon when his Ass spoke; for I find just as People please or displease us in this World, we accordingly assign them a Place of Happiness or Unhappiness in the next. Vertue shall be rewarded and Vice punished hereafter, it's true, but when, or how, I believe every Man knows as well as the Pope; therefore many People have blam'd the Inscription of your Marble, and think it a presumption in the Pen-man to be so very positive in matters, which the wisest of Mankind, without death, can come to no true knowledge of. The Fanaticks especially are very highly offended at it, and say, it looks as if a Man could Toot himself to Heaven upon the Whore of *Babylon's* Bagpipes, and that Religion consists only in the true setting of a Catch, or composing of a Madrigal. I have had many a bitter squabble with them in defence of your Epitaph, upon which they scoffingly advis'd me to get Monsieur *de-Urfey* to Tag it with Rhime, and then my self to Garnish it with a Tune, and so make it a Catch in imitation of *Under this Stone lies* Gabriel John, *&c.* which unlucky saying so Dumbfounded me, that I was forc'd silently to submit, because you had serv'd with another Person's Epitaph after the same manner.

I have no Novelties to entertain you with relating to either the *Abby* or St. *Pauls,* for both the Quires continue just as wicked as they were when you left them; some of them dayly come wrecking hot out of a Bawdy-House into the Church; and others Stagger out of a Tavern to Afternoon-Prayers, and Hickup over a little of the Littany, and so back again. Old Carret-Face beats time still upon his Cushion stoutly, and sits growling under his Purple Canopy a hearty old-fashioned Base that deafens all about him. Beau Bushy-Whig preserves his Voice to a miracle, Charms all the Ladies over against him with his handsome Face; and all over Head with his Singing. Parson Punch makes a very good shift still, and Lyricks over his part in an Anthem very handsomly. So much for the Church; and now for the Play-houses, which are grown so abominably wicked since the pious Society have undertook to reform them, that not a Member of the Fraternity will sit down to his Dinner, till he has repeated over a Catalogue of Curses upon the Crew of Sin-sucking Hippocrites, as long as a Presbyterian Grace, then falls to with a good Appetite, and Damns them as heartily after Dinner; nor will they begin a Play upon the Stage, unless Larded with half a dozen lushous Bawdy Songs in contempt of Reforming Authority, some Writ by Mr. *C*____ and Set by your Friend Doctor *B*____; others Writ by Mr. *D*____, and Set by your Friend Mr. *E*____: You know Men of our Profession hang between the Church and the Play-house, as *Mahomet's* Tomb does between the two Load-Stones, and must equally incline to both, because by both we are equally supported.

Religion is grown a Stalking-horse to every Bodies Interest, and every Man chuses to be of that Faith which he finds to be most profitable. Our Parochial-Churches this hot Weather are but indifferently fill'd, but our Cathedrals are still crowded as they us'd to be, because to One that comes thither truly to serve God, fifty come purely to hear the Musick; the Blessing of Peace has again quite forsaken us, and the People, tired with being Happy, have drawn the Curse of War upon their own Heads; and the Clergy, like true Christians, confound their Enemies heartily. Money begins already to be as scarce as Truth, Honour and Honesty; and a Man may walk from *Ludgate* to *Aldgate* near high Change time, and not meet a Citizen with a full Bag under his Arm, or a jot of plain dealing in his Conscience: The Ready *Specie* lies all in the Bank and the Exchequer, and most Traders Estates lie in their Pocket Books and their Comb cases: Paper goes current instead of Cash, and Pen and Ink does us more service than the Mines in the *Indies*. I am very much in Arrears upon the account of my Business, as well as the Brethren of my Quality; but whether we shall be paid in this World or the next, we are none of us yet certain. You made a timely step out of a troublesome World, could I imagine you were got into a Worse, I could easily pin my Faith upon impossibilities; but fare as you will, it cannot be long e'er I shall give you my company,

and discover the truth of that which our Priests talk so much of and know
so little:

Till then I rest yours
B_____[1]

IX

'The devine Purcell' – Purcell recalled

THOMAS TUDWAY

(c. 1650–1726)

The career of the English composer and organist Thomas
Tudway was centred on Cambridge, where he was organist
of King's College from 1670, and from then until 1680
Master of the Choristers. In 1705 he was appointed Professor
of Music in the university. His early years had been spent in
the Chapel Royal and, since his voice broke in 1668, probably
overlapped with Purcell's first years there. When Robert,
Lord Harley, asked him to compile a collection of cathedral
music, a task which occupied him from 1714 to 1720, he
appended short notes on the music, including one for Purcell.

I knew him perfectly well. He had a most commendable ambition of
exceeding every one of his time, and he succeeded in it without contradic-
tion, there being none in England, nor anywhere else that I know of,
that could come into competition with him for compositions of all kinds.
Towards the latter end of his life he was prevailed on to compose for the
English stage. There was nothing that ever had appeared in England like
the representations he made of all kinds, whether of pomp or solemnity,
in his grand chorus, etc., or that exquisite piece called the freezing piece
of musick; in representing a mad couple, or country swains making love,
or indeed any other kind of music whatever. But these are trifles in
comparison of the solemn pieces he made for the Church, in which I will
name but one, and that is his *Te Deum, &c.*, with instruments, a composition for skill and invention beyond what was ever attempted in England
before his time.[1]

UNIVERSAL JOURNAL

The unsigned article in the form of a letter which appeared
in the *Universal Journal* in 1724 echoes the sentiments found
in works by Macky and Defoe; that is, the 1720s marked a
decline in the number of performances of Purcell's works,
Handel and the new Italian style were more popular and the
century, in the search for things new, was in danger of
abandoning its great Orpheus. Such expressions also indicate

a growing interest in 'ancient music', an interest central to such eighteenth-century institutions as the Academy of Ancient Music.

To the Author of the Universal Journal.

SIR,

AS you seem, by some of your Writings, to bear Respect to the Memory of the late famous Mr. *Henry Purcel*, it has revived my Veneration for that wonderful Man, and stirr'd up a little Resentment in me against the modern Fops, who seem resolv'd to tear the Laurel from his Brow, and lay his Memory low in Oblivion.

I shall not vindicate him at the Expence of any Musician now living, tho' I hope I may without Offence, say, That *Purcel* was a *Shakespear* in *Musick*; and tho' we have had many great Poets since *Shakespear*, yet as none have exceeded, may I not say equal'd him; so tho' Musick has been improved almost to a Prodigy since *Purcel's* Time, yet those Lines of Mr. *Hall's* may be very well apply'd.

> *Sometimes a Hero in an Age appears;*
> *But scarce a* Purcel *in a Thousand Years.*

Now that this Great Man's Fame should dye, nay worse, that his incomparable Works should be made a Jest of by ignorant Coxcombs, who praise and condemn but by Example, and for Fashion's Sake, is enough to raise Resentment in any, who have the least Regard to the Honour of their Country, or Concern for true Merit.

The first and chief Reflection they cast on his Musick, is, that 'tis Old Stile: I grant it; (all the World knows it was not made Yesterday;) but I cannot comprehend these Gentlemans nice Distinction of Old Stile and New Stile, unless they would infer that the three Sister-Arts never flourished 'till now, or that the Musick, Painting and Poetry of the last Age is Old Stile, (*i.e.*) out of Date, and therefore ought to be kick'd out of Doors.

We have doubtless many good Painters now living; must therefore *Rubens*, *Vandyke*, *Lilly* and *Kneller* be forgot? Must *Spencer*, *Milton*, *Shakespear*, and *Addison* be never read, because there are Writers of a later Date? And must *Corelli*, *Bird*, and *Purcel* never be sung, because they are Old Stile?

In Musick we have many Great Masters now living, to support the

Dignity of that heavenly Science; but it is the worst Complement any one can pay them, to make Blockheads of *Corelli* and *Purcel*. I am confident they would receive it with as much Indignation as Mr. *Pope* or Mr. *Phillips* would hear a Reflection on *Shakespear*, tho' never so much intended in their Favour. No, 'tis only the noisy Vulgar who set up Idols, and demolish the Shrines of the Ancients. It is from our present Great Men I would have our *petits Maitres* silenced.

I defy any Person living to have a greater Veneration for *Raphael*, *Rubens*, and *Vandyke*, than *Richardson*, *Drake*, or *Vandebank* have for those glorious Ancients. Let our Dabblers in Poetry therefore learn of *Philips* or *Welsted* to prize *Milton*: And had every Man the same Value for our *Purcel*, as the wonderful *Hendel* has, I had never set Pen to Paper. In Co[n]temporaries indeed Emulation may eclipse the Merit of great Men in each other's Opinion: But the Grave throws all Blots aside; and there can be little Merit, where there is not Generosity enough to have Respect to the good Works of our Ancestors.

Purcel was our great Reformer of Musick; he had a most happy enterprizing Genius, join'd with a boundless Invention, and noble Design. He made Musick answer its Ends (*i.e.*) move the Passions. He express'd his Words with a singular Beauty and Energy; there is a Manliness of Stile [that] runs through his Works; and were *Italian* Words put to one of his Airs, they would not be found Old Stile, nor need any of our modern Composers be ashamed of them.

His Recitative is gracefully natural, and particularly adapted to the *English* Tongue. There is a Solemnity in his Songs, which at the same time awes and pleases; and when they do not, the Fault is too frequently either in the Singer, who consults not the Intention of the Author, or in the Hearer who is determined to condemn whatever is *Purcel's*.

Had that great Man lived till now, he had doubtless made yet greater Improvements in Musick; and it must be owned a great Misfortune, that his Works were not corrected by himself, but after his Death all Copies were called in from private Hands, and a Collection made with a View more to the Bookseller's Advantage, than the Author's Honour. There are doubtless many Songs in *Orpheus Britannicus*, which *Purcel* never intended for the Publick; little Occasional Pieces, done in his Juvenile Years, which he never designed to transmit to Posterity. But then, on the contrary, there are in that very Book, (and of those a great many) such bright Originals, as will outlive the Malice and Ignorance of this fantas-

tick Generation, and shine to the latest Posterity; when the Memory of
that glorious *Englishman* shall again flourish, and when Musick and
Reason shall once more be united.[2]

OLIVER GOLDSMITH
(1728–74)

The Irish playwright Oliver Goldsmith's early career was
somewhat chequered, and culminated in a penniless 'grand
tour' on foot as a flute-playing busker. By the late 1750s he
was gaining renown as a writer, but he died of fever the year
after the first production of his most successful work, *She
Stoops to Conquer*. His essay on national styles in music
appeared in the *British Magazine* in 1760.

It is worthy [of] remark, in general, that the music of every country is
solemn, in proportion as the inhabitants are merry . . . Thus, in France,
Poland, Ireland, and Switzerland, the national music is slow, melancholy,
and solemn; in Italy, England, Spain, and Germany, it is faster, pro-
portionably as the people are grave. Lully only changed a bad manner,
which he found, for a bad one of his own. His drowsy pieces are played
still to the most sprightly audience that can be conceived; and even though
Rameau, who is at once a musician and a philosopher, has shewn, both
by precept and example, what improvements French music may still
admit of, yet his countrymen seem little convinced by his reasonings; and
the Pont-Neuf taste, as it is called, still prevails in their best performances.

The English School was first planned by Purcel: he attempted to unite
the Italian manner, that prevailed in his time, with the ancient Celtic
carrol and the Scotch ballad, which probably had also its origins in Italy:
for some of the best Scotch ballads (the Broom of Cowdenknows, for
instance) are still ascribed to David Rizzio. But be that as it will, his
manner was something peculiar to the English; and he might have continued as head of the English school, had not his merits been entirely
eclipsed by Handel. Handel, though originally a German, yet adopted
the English manner: he had long laboured to please by Italian composition,
but without success; and though his English oratorios are accounted inimi-
table, yet his Italian operas are fallen into oblivion.[3]

CHARLES BURNEY
(1726–1814)

As the English music historian and composer Charles Burney
toured extensively on the Continent, he compiled two volumes
of what are essentially expanded travel diaries. He was collect-
ing material in preparation for the writing of his *magnum
opus*, *A General History of Music*, which appeared in four
volumes between 1776 and 1789. His assessment of Purcell
is extensive and includes a consideration of a large number
of works. The verdict is not entirely favourable to Purcell,
though Burney believes his shortcomings were due to his
being born in the wrong century.

Unluckily for Purcell! he built his fame with such perishable materials,
that his worth and works are daily diminishing, while the reputation of
our poets and philosophers is increasing by the constant study and use of
their productions. And so much is our great musician's celebrity already
consigned to tradition, that it will soon be as difficult to find his songs,
or, at least to *hear* them, as those of his predecessors, Orpheus and
Amphion, with which Cerberus was lulled to sleep, or the city of Thebes
constructed.

So changeable is taste in Music, and so transient the favour of any
particular style, that its history is like that of a ploughed field: such a year
it produced wheat, such a year barley, peas, or clover; and such a year
lay fallow. But none of its productions remain, except, perhaps, a finall
part of last year's crop, and the corn or weeds that now cover its surface.
Purcell, however, was such an excellent cultivator of his farm in Par-
nassus, that its crops will be long remembered, even after time has
devoured them . . .

The superior genius of Purcell can be fairly estimated only by those
who make themselves acquainted with the state of Music previous to the
time in which he flourished; compared with which, his productions for
the Church, if not more learned, will be found infinitely more varied and
expressive; and his secular compositions appear to have descended from
another more happy region, with which neither his predecessors nor
cotemporaries had any commu[ni]cation . . .

And now, having heartily praised Purcell's extensive genius and talents,

I shall not dissemble his defects. Melody, during his short existence, was not sufficiently polished by great fingers; and though there are grand designs in his works, and masterly strokes of composition and expression, yet his melody wants symmetry and grace. And by writing on a given base, which forced him to submit to a crude, and sometimes a licentious and unwarrantable use of passing-notes, his harmony is not always so pure as it ought to be. However, in all his Music that has been printed, except the compositions for the church, of which Dr. Boyce superintended the impression, errors of the press are innumerable, which must not be charged to his account.

An absurd custom prevailed in Purcell's time, which he carried to greater excess, perhaps, than any other composer, of repeating a word of one or two syllables an unlimitted number of times, for the sake of the melody, and sometimes before the whole sentence has been heard. Such as no, no, no – all, all, all – pretty, pretty, pretty, &c. *ad infinitum.*

He was so little acquainted with the unlimited powers of the violin, that I have scarcely ever seen a becoming passage for that instrument in any one of his works; the symphonies and ritornels to his anthems and songs being equally deficient in force, invention, and effect. And though his sonatas contain many ingenious, and, at the time they were composed, new traits of melody and modulation, if they are compared with the productions of his cotemporary, Corelli, they will be called barbarous. But Corelli wrote for an instrument of which he was a great master: and who ever entirely succeeded in composing for one of which he was ignorant? When a great performer on keyed-instruments condescends to compose for the violin, upon which he has never been a good player, or the voice, without knowing in what good singing consists, the passages all come from the head and none from the hand, except the hand of a harpsichord player, which is ever unfit to suggest ideas either for a voice or for any other instrument than his own. Such a composer for the violin must inevitably embarrass the player with perpetual aukwardnesses and difficulties without effect, which discover an utter ignorance of the finger-board.

If Purcell, by travelling, or by *living longer* at home, had heard the great instrumental performers, as well as great singers, that arrived in this country soon after his decease, and had had such to compose for, his productions would have been more regular, elegant, and graceful; and he would certainly have set *English words* better than it was possible for any foreigner to do, for our feelings, however great his genius, or excellent, in other respects, his productions. But Purcell, like his successor, Arne, and others who have composed for the playhouse, had always an inferior band to the Italian opera composers, as well as inferior singers, and an inferior audience, to write for.

The diligent and candid Walther, by not having assigned to Purcell a niche in his Musical Dictionary, seems never to have heard of his existence; but Purcell was so truly a *national* composer, that his name was not likely to be wafted to the continent; and the narrow limits of his fame may be fairly ascribed, not only to the paucity and poverty of his compositions for instruments, for which the musical productions are an intelligible language to every country, but to his vocal compositions being solely adapted to English words, which rendered it unlikely for their influence to extend beyond the soil that produced them . . .

Let those who shall think Purcell has sacrificed the national honour by confessing his reverence for the productions of Italy, compare the secular productions of English musicians, from the death of Queen Elizabeth to the year 1683, with those of Carissimi, Cesti, Stradella, and innumerable others of great abilities, and if they do not equally hate Music and truth, they will admire Purcell's probity, as well as his genius.

Indeed, Music was manifestly on the decline, in England, during the seventeenth century, till it was revived and invigorated by Purcell, whose genius, though less cultivated and polished, was equal to that of the greatest masters on the continent. And though his dramatic style and recitative were formed in a great measure on French models, there is a latent power and force in his expression of English words, whatever be the subject, that will make an unprejudiced native of this island feel, more than all the elegance, grace, and refinement of modern Music less happily applied, can do. And this pleasure is communicated to us, not by the symmetry or rhythm of modern melody, but by his having fortified, lengthened, and tuned, the true accents of our mother-tongue; those notes of passion, which an inhabitant of this island would breathe, in such situations as the words he has to set, describe. And these indigenous expressions of passion Purcell has the power to enforce by the energy of modulation, which, on some occasions, was bold, affecting, and sublime.[4]

GERARD MANLEY HOPKINS
(1844–89)

The career of the Roman Catholic poet Gerard Manley Hopkins was distinguished by the fact that none of his poems was published during his lifetime. After early years spent variously at Highgate School, Balliol College, Oxford, and Stonyhurst he became Professor of Greek at Trinity College, Dublin, in 1884. By contrast, his close Oxford friend Robert Bridges (1844–1930) published poetry from 1873, and was appointed Poet Laureate in 1913. Bridges brought out the posthumous collection of Hopkins's poems that included his sonnet 'Henry Purcell'.

Henry Purcell

The poet wishes well to the divine genius of Purcell and praises him that, whereas other musicians have given utterance to the moods of man's mind, he has, beyond that, uttered in notes the very make and species of man as created both in him and in all men generally.

Have fair fallen, O fair, fair have fallen, so dear
To me, so arch-especial a spirit as heaves in Henry Purcell,
An age is now since passed, since parted; with the reversal
Of the outward sentence low lays him, listed to a heresy, here.

Not mood in him nor meaning, proud fire or sacred fear,
Or love, or pity, or all that sweet notes not his might nursle:
It is the forgèd feature finds me; it is the rehearsal
Of own, of abrupt self there so thrusts on, so throngs the ear.

Let him Oh! with his air of angels then lift me, lay me! only I'll
Have an eye to the sakes of him, quaint moonmarks, to his pelted
    plumage under
Wings: so some great stormfowl, whenever he has walked his while

The thunder-purple seabeach, plumèd purple-of-thunder,
If a wuthering of his palmy snow-pinions scatter a colossal smile
Off him, but meaning motion fans fresh our wits with wonder.[5]

Hopkins and Bridges maintained a regular correspondence,
in which Hopkins had this to say on the sonnet and its
meaning:

The sestet of the Purcell sonnet is not so clearly worked out as I could
wish. The thought is that as the seabird opening his wings with a whiff
of wind in your face means the whirr of the motion, but also unawares
gives you a whiff of knowledge about his plumage, the marking of which
stamps his species, that he does not mean, so Purcell, seemingly intent
only on the thought or feeling he is to express or call out, incidentally
lets you remark the individualising marks of his own genius.[6]

By the by your remark on Purcell's music does not conflict with what my
sonnet says, rather it supports it. My sonnet means 'Purcell's music is
none of your d—d subjective rot' (so to speak). Read it again.[7]

The sonnet on Purcell means this: 1–4. I hope Purcell is not damned for
being a Protestant, because I love his genius. 5–8. And that not so much
for gifts he shares, even though it shd. be in higher measure, with other
musicians as for his own individuality. 9–14. So that while he is aiming
only at impressing me his hearer with the meaning in hand I am looking
out meanwhile for his specific, his individual markings and mottlings,
'the sakes of him'. It is as when a bird thinking only of soaring spreads
its wings: a beholder may happen then to have his attention drawn by the
act to the plumage displayed. – In particular, the first lines mean: May
Purcell, O may he have died a good death and that soul which I love so
much and which breathes or stirs so unmistakeably in his works have
parted from the body and passed away, centuries since though I frame
the wish, in peace with God! so that the heavy condemnation under which
he outwardly or nominally lay for being out of the true Church may in
consequence of his good intentions have been reversed. 'Low lays him' is
merely 'lays him low', that is/strikes him heavily, weighs upon him. (I
daresay this will strike you as more professional than you had anticipated.)
It is somewhat dismaying to find I am so unintelligible though, especially
in one of my very best pieces. 'Listed', by the by, is 'enlisted'. 'Sakes' is
hazardous: about that point I was more bent on saying my say than on
being understood in it. The 'moonmarks' belong to the image only of
course, not to the application; I mean not detailedly: I was thinking of a
bird's quill feathers. One thing disquiets me: *I meant* 'fair fall' to mean

fair (fortune be) fall; it has since struck me that perhaps 'fair' is an adjective proper and in the predicate and can only be used in cases like 'fair fall the day', that is, *may the day fall, turn out, fair*. My line will yield a sense that way indeed, but I never meant it so. Do you know any passage decisive on this?

Would that I had Purcell's music here.[8]

GEORGE BERNARD SHAW

Although George Bernard Shaw is best known to Purcellians for his review of *Dido and Aeneas* (see p. 80), Purcell flits across the pages of his musical criticism, revealing Shaw's unalloyed appreciation of the composer. On the subject of the need for a revitalization of musical life in England, of which he was keenly aware, Shaw cites Purcell as an unattainable ideal.

We cannot count on another Purcell; but in my opinion England's turn in art is coming, especially since there is a growing disposition among us to carry our social aims further than providing every middle-class dog with his own manger as soon as he is able to pay for it.[9]

And, perhaps not entirely accurately when the general standard of the language Purcell set is considered, on Purcell's probable preference for Walter Scott over the ineffable Julian Sturgiss, librettist of Sullivan's Scot-opera *Ivanhoe*, he writes:

If the noble dialogue of Scott is not more suitable for English Music than the fustian of Mr. Sturgis, then so much the worse for English music. Purcell would have found it so. I protest, in the name of my own art of letters, against a Royal English Opera which begins by handing over a literary masterpiece for wanton debasement at the hands of a journeyman hired for the job.[10]

Most perceptive, however, are his comments on the second viol concert organized by the early-music exponent Arnold Dolmetsch (1858–1940).

Mr Dolmetsch has taken up an altogether un-English position in this matter. He says 'Purcell was a great composer: let us perform some of his works'. The English musicians say 'Purcell was a great composer: let

us go and do Mendelssohn's Elijah over again and make the Lord-
lieutenant of the country chairman of the committee.'[11]

THREE BICENTENARY TRIBUTES

Musical Times

The influential music critic and writer Joseph Bennett
(1831–1911) started his journalistic career as an assistant on
the *Sunday Times*; he moved to the *Daily Telegraph* in 1870
and remained there until his retirement in 1906. He was also
on the staff of the *Musical Times*, in which he published a
tribute to Purcell.

That is not a perfect state of things in which past greatness comes to
honour chiefly through the agency of times and seasons. It should always
be so present as not to need the help of an almanack. But, on the other
hand, we have cause to be thankful when times and seasons bring to mind
that which otherwise, perhaps, we should overlook, or discern so faintly
as to fall short of due homage. Hence all reflecting men welcome the
approaching bi-centenary of Purcell's death as an opportunity of making
known to the ignorant or careless how fine a genius passed away two
hundred years ago . . .

   I could not, by ever so much and so careful quotation from Purcell's
works, convey a complete idea of their wealth in the highest and subtlest
qualities of music. Quotation, indeed, might tend to false conclusions,
because of a now antiquated outward and visible form. The spirit of
which I speak is changeless, serving for all time, and comes nearest to us
not when in critical mood we examine the text, but when, listening with
open souls, we pass under the influence of the master's genius. True, we
do not all hear with the same ears, or with the same measure of freedom
from prejudice – that disturbing and misleading element without which
every man would, more or less, see good. In this matter we must individu-
ally act according to the light that is in us, and, for myself, I say that,
despite much in Purcell's works which belongs to the fashion of the time,
and much other hardly to be classed as specially distinctive, I know
scarcely one example absolutely wanting in the note of genius – in that
sublime trumpet call which summons every hearer to attention, and
subdues him to its will.[12]

Illustrated London News

The *Illustrated London News* devoted an impressive amount of
lavishly illustrated space to the composer for the bicentenary.
Pictures include Purcell's tablet, his house in Bowling Alley
and Westminster Abbey. A journal of flattery rather than
serious critical analysis, its tone is typical of the later nineteenth-century writing on the composer.

It is just two hundred years ago, this month of November, since Purcell
died in the thirty-seventh year of his age, and was buried beneath the
organ in Westminster Abbey. He had more than a touch of genius. Not
only did he compose the most beautiful anthems that are sung in our
cathedrals, but he composed a 'Te Deum' worthy of Handel; and with
him rests the honour of writing the first English opera . . . He was an
infant prodigy; and had the booming of infant prodigies been a profession
in those days, the lad would have been the fortune of some enterprising
agent. It is believed that he composed at the age of nine . . . The organist
of Westminster Abbey at that time was Dr. John Blow, a loving, appreciative man, who soon recognised the genius of his pupil. His appreciation
went so far that he actually resigned his office that Purcell might be the
organist of the majestic old pile . . . To commemorate this great master
of English church music . . . one of his anthems has been included in
the service every week at Westminster this year. There is to be a service
on the anniversary of Purcell's death, and the music which first found
voice in the old Abbey will be echoed again in all its majesty and grand
simplicity.[13]

Monthly Music Record

The *Monthly Music Record* was, until its demise in December
1960, edited anonymously. Its editor in 1895, however,
seems to have been J. S. Shedlock (1843–1919), the English
pianist and writer on music who is chiefly known to Purcellians as the editor of the Purcell Society's first *Fairy-Queen*.
His description of the bicentenary activity offers some salutary
comments equally applicable in 1995.

So much has been written, so much more is being written, about Purcell,
his life, and his works, that we have no desire to weary our readers with
a fresh account of them, differing from previous accounts only in language
and in arrangement of petty detail. Further, the interest aroused in Purcell

by the recent Commemoration concerts seemed slight, transient, easily
spent. It will slumber, we greatly fear, for another century at least, unless,
indeed, sixty-three years hence, while this generation sleeps its final sleep,
some few ardent souls go out to keep sacred the three-hundredth anniversary of Purcell's birth. Meantime, we have no wish to act the part of the
public conscience. The English have all but forgotten Purcell, and quite
forgotten the greatness of the work he did. That is their loss, and theirs
only. Purcell is secure; his work stands fast. And our object in thinking
of him at the present moment is not to repeat the old, old stories, nor to
reproach the public with their neglect of the subject of those stories; but
to point, at a time when it is acknowledged that Purcell did achieve
something, to a part of the secret of his artistic success. The major part
of that secret was his genius, as all know who know Purcell.[14]

DONALD FRANCIS TOVEY

(1875–1940)

> The critic, composer and pianist Donald Francis Tovey,
> famed for his elegant and perceptive musical criticism, was
> for many years Reid Professor of Music at the University of
> Edinburgh. His appreciation of Purcell was not uncritical,
> but his warmth shines through his discussions of the compos-
> er's skills in his essays 'The Main Stream of Music' and
> 'Musical Textures'.

Early in the seventeenth century the violins ousted the flat-backed nasal-
toned family of viols, and instrumental music began to assert itself. The
harpsichord was already, in its early form of spinet and virginals, a
resourceful instrument that amused William Byrd and other great Tudor
composers. Queen Elizabeth herself condescended to be a great virtuoso
in keyboard music; and English patriotism does not outrun discretion if
we claim that this interesting backwater – the instrumental music of the
sixteenth century – was thoroughly explored by English composers. The
healthiness of a backwater depends upon its access to the main stream
and its immunity from the encroachments of the Corporation dump.
Unfortunately, the subsequent history of English music up to recent times
has been a deplorable story of frustration, stagnation, and drifting into
silted-up channels. There are periods in which it may be fairly said that

English music has itself consisted of the Corporation dump. Our greatest
musical genius, Henry Purcell, was born either fifty years too soon or
fifty years too late: too late to be a master of the Golden Age, now that
instrumental music had flooded out every landmark of Palestrina's art:
too early to gain command of the future resources of Bach and Handel.
His opera *Dido and Aeneas*, written for the pupils of Mr Josiah Priest's
boarding-school, with a libretto by Nahum Tate, of the firm of Tate and
Brady, achieves musical coherence and anticipates every quality of the
operas in which Gluck reformed dramatic music nearly a century later.
If Purcell had been allowed to write more operas on such lines he would
have carried a recognizable main stream of music through all the tangle
of mountain-torrents and parched arroyos which the musical historian
finds so interesting in the eighteenth century, but which is so distressing to
the searcher for mature masterpieces who is not deceived by the nineteenth-
century cookery which makes the *disjecta membra* of seventeenth-century
music palatable to the concert singer. To anyone who realizes what might
have been achieved for and by Purcell, the honoured name of glorious
John Dryden deserves always to be accompanied by a heartfelt recitation
of the 109th Psalm. That completely unmusical time-server began by
insulting Purcell and other gifted English musicians in a panegyric of an
obviously incompetent Monsieur Grabu, whom King Charles II had
foolishly set at the head of his court musicians, and whose work proved
more perishable than waste paper. A few years later Dryden mended his
manners towards Purcell in his public utterances, but proceeded to dam
the whole future current of English dramatic music by ordaining that the
music of his operas should be confined to characters outside the real action
of his plays. Thus, even when Dryden condescends to adapt Shakespeare's
Tempest, he contrives that Purcell's music for it shall have nothing to do
with Shakespeare. And what should have been Purcell's most important
work, *King Arthur*, has not the smallest chance of taking shape as a
coherent musical scheme. We not only accepted the consequences of
Dryden's Philistinism throughout the next century, but imposed them
with murderous results upon one of the greatest dramatic composers of
the early nineteenth century, Weber, who found, when he had already
committed himself to writing an opera for the English stage, that the
librettist, Planché, neither knew nor cared to learn that a composer of
dramatic music was concerned with the coherence of a music-drama as a
whole. Planché cheerfully said, 'And now we will show them what we

can do next time'; but it was already obvious that Weber's time was fully occupied in dying of rapid consumption.

We can hardly doubt that, if the musical resources of Bach and Handel had been at Purcell's command, his genius would have had the power to break through the bonds of the Philistines, and in fact I know no other case where musical genius has come into the world so manifestly at the wrong time and place, without having found the opportunity to develop some other art or science more ready for the work of a great mind. For we cannot doubt that a talent for music, in spite of its highly special nature, is part of a very much larger general ability which has become concentrated upon music by circumstances less normal than we are apt to suppose.[15]

Present me with a perfect performance of Schütz's *Lamentatio Davidi*, with a first-rate singer, four trombones, and an organ, and ask me to judge by its purely musical values when it was written. I have no means of knowing that it was not written the day before yesterday by Holst or Vaughan Williams in a mood of inspiration which happened to exclude both the more modern and the more deliberately archaic features of their styles. Present me with almost any random short quotation from Purcell, and I would guess that this must be by some composer of the calibre of Bach or Handel, though evidently neither of those masters. From a short quotation, I could certainly not guess the lamentable fact that Purcell was almost always prevented from building a coherent work of art on a large scale. It is a fascinating occupation to roam through the music of the seventeenth century in search of beautiful and stimulating passages; but the connoisseur whose favourite period in music is the seventeenth century is farther from the truth than one who accepts the comparatively philistine judgement that between the death of Palestrina in 1594 and the birth of Bach and Handel in 1685 there are no great composers.[16]

BRITAIN, 1951

The Arts Council's contribution to the Festival of Britain was a distinguished one. Apart from the expected support of individual events, the Council itself promoted three concert series of English music. Of the one devoted to Purcell *The Times* wrote:

When the new club of the International Music Association was opened in London the other day it was musically baptized with a performance of one of Purcell's shorter St Cecilia Odes. Nothing could have been more suitable not only for the semi-private occasion but for the music itself, for the large public concert does not easily accommodate Henry Purcell, who lived and worked when social conditions as a *milieu* for music were very different from today's.

Much of Purcell's music is domestic music, and as such can still find employment in the home and will travel over the radio to the fireside in good shape. The church music has never altogether lost its place in the Church, though changing fashions of taste have subjected it to adverse criticism from time to time. But both the occasional music and the theatrical music present obstacles to modern revival because there are neither occasions nor theatres for which they are suitable. On the other hand not many symphony concerts can find a place for an overture, a suite, or a chaconne of Purcell's dramatic music, and choral societies find the St. Cecilia's Day Odes too insubstantial and *King Arthur* too scrappy for their ordinary concerts of oratorio dimensions. For this reason, the present series of eight Purcell concerts at the Victoria and Albert Museum has been designed with the specific intention of overcoming the mere misfitting circumstances. The circumstantial attachments to the seventeenth century have also been cut away and the larger music adapted to concert purposes. Its immense vitality immediately asserts itself when so presented, and shows us what we miss by our neglect of a great national treasure.[17]

JACK WESTRUP
(1904–75)

Sir Jack Westrup, Heather Professor of Music at Oxford (1947–71), was chairman of the Purcell Society from 1957 until his death in 1975. His account of Purcell's life and music, first published in 1937, has, with revisions, remained the standard text on the composer. For the tercentenary of Purcell's birth he penned a short article for the *Musical Times* on Purcell's reputation.

Purcell's music has always been admired by discerning musicians, but it has not always been well known. Even today, when the Purcell Society's protracted edition approaches completion, there is a great deal that is rarely, if ever, performed. Singers are too often content to repeat the same handful of songs, generally in poor and out-of-date editions, or if they show more enterprise tend to squander it on 'realizations' which run counter to the spirit of the music and the age in which it was written. Orchestras play arrangements of theatre music in which gratuitous wind parts have been grafted on to Purcell's wonderful writing for strings. Cathedral choirs happily perpetuate numerous errors to be found in ancient copies from which they sing. This is partly due to the lack of initiative shown by publishers. The Purcell Society's edition is a treasure house of music waiting to be discovered by performers; but the volumes are not very convenient for practical use, and in any case most of them have been out of print for several years.[18]

X

Composers on Purcell – Purcell regain'd

ARCANGELO CORELLI
(1653–1713)

The unflattering view of the influential composer Arcangelo
Corelli survives, unfortunately, only second-hand. Corelli's
career was notable, for it did not rely on the opera house, and
his reputation owed much to the activities of music publishers.
Further, like some of Purcell's music, his compositions
became 'ancient musick', being performed after the style in
which they were written was no longer fashionable.

It is [ ] ridiculous to criticise an opera as a puppet-show or I could send
you over a Long Catalogue of the like Indecencys: but since I have
mention'd Musick I can't forbear telling you that Corelli has a very mean
opinion of Harry Purcell's works as a gentleman told me that presented
them to him, which I suppose Will be no Small Mortification to You
Tramontane composers.[1]

GEORGE FREDERICK HANDEL
(1685–1759)

The German-born composer G. F. Handel, like Purcell, has
only a small number of anecdotes attributed to him. R. J. S.
Stevens (1757–1837), organist, antiquarian and, from 1801,
Gresham Professor of Music, included Handel's appreciation
of Purcell in his collection of anecdotes; he even couched it
in Handel's German accent.

When Handel was blind, and attending a performance of the oratorio of
Jephtha, Mr. Savage (my master) who sat next to him, said, 'This movement, sir, reminds me of some of Purcell's old music.' 'O got te teffel'
(said Handel). 'If Purcell had lived he would have composed better music
than this.'[2]

HENRY CAREY

(*c.* 1690–1743)

Carey, a talented critic, poet and composer, was the author
of numerous songs, dramatic pieces and poems. Some of
his later poems, such as 'The Poet's Resentment', suggest a
bitterness of his constant failure to achieve both a reputation
and a steady income. Foreign imports – probably the Italian
opera with which he had competed in the early 1730s – are
his target here. That Purcell's music appears to be held in
similar contempt is offered by Carey as a measure of the
decline.

The Poet's Resentment

RESIGN thy Pipe! thy wonted lays forego;
The Muse is now become thy greatest Foe:
With Taunts and Jeers, and most unfriendly wrongs,
The flouting Rabble pay thee for thy Songs.
Untuneful is our Native Language now;
Nor must the Bays adorn a *British* Brow:
The wanton Vulgar scorn their Mother-Tongue,
And all our home-bred Bards have bootless sung.
A false Politness has possess'd the Isle,
And ev'ry Thing that's *English* is Old Stile.

Ev'n Heav'n-born PURCEL now is held in Scorn,
PURCEL! who did a brighter Age adorn.
That nobleness of Soul, that Martial Fire,
Which did our BRITISH ORPHEUS once inspire
To rouze us all to Arms, is quite forgot;
We aim at something . . . but we know not what:
Effeminate in Dress, in Manners grown
We now despise whatever is our Own.[3]

WILLIAM BOYCE
(1711–79)

Like Tudway, William Boyce was a composer, organist and collector of cathedral music, but his volumes were widely disseminated and maintained his reputation during the nineteenth century. His career was spent in a variety of posts, including organist of St Michael's Cornhill, and in 1757 he was sworn in as Master of the King's Musick. His short assessment of Purcell is to be found in the second volume of *Cathedral Music*.

He appears to have possessed a Genius superior to any of his Predecessors, together with a depth of Musical Knowledge not inferior to the most learned of them. His Talents were not confined to any particular Manner or Stile of Composition, for he was equally excellent in every thing he attempted; and it is doing but common Justice to his Memory to acknowledge, that his Works, in general, affect more powerfully, than those of almost any other Author.[4]

JOHN STAFFORD SMITH
(1750–1836)

A pupil of Boyce, John Stafford Smith was successively a chorister and Gentleman of the Chapel Royal, and from 1805 to 1817, Master of the Children. He not only collected manuscripts, but also published much early music, and is considered the first English musicologist. His *Collection of English Songs*, in which his remarks on Purcell appear, is thought by Nicholas Temperley to be 'the first scholarly edition printed in England'.

Mr. *Purcel* has been heard to declare more than once, that the *Variety* which the *minor Key* is capable of affording, by the Change of Sounds in the ascending and descending Scale, induced him so frequently to give it the Preference; and this Variety seems to have tempted some, even after him, to continue the Practice of the Mode-Style. In the Church Service particularly, the Solemnity and Dignity of this Style should never be lost.[5]

C. HUBERT H. PARRY
(1848–1918)

Sir Hubert Parry exerted a forceful, invigorating influence on England's musical life at a time when it was moribund and standards were suspect. Director of the Royal College of Music, Choragus in the University of Oxford, a contributor to the first of George Grove's music dictionaries and a holder of honorary degrees from Cambridge, Oxford and Durham, he was created a baronet for his services to music. His scholarly activities were multifarious and did much to restore the flagging intellectual fortunes of English music, though they were not wholly favourable to Purcell.

In the late phase of the madrigal period, which was almost exclusively centred in England, composers aimed at characteristic expression of the words far oftener than the great Italian masters had done; and they often showed that tendency towards realistic expression which Purcell carried to such an excess. Purcell was indeed the greatest musical genius of his age, but his lines were cast in most unfortunate places. His circumstances put him completely out of touch with the choral methods of the great period; and the standards and models for the new style, and the examples of what could and what could not be done, were so deficient that his judgment went constantly astray; and in trying to carry out his ideals according to the principles of the 'new music' he occasionally achieves a marvellous stroke of real genius, and not unfrequently falls into the depths of bathos and childishness. The experiments which he made in expression, under the same impulse as Schütz in church choral music, are quite astounding in crudeness, and almost impossible to sing; while in secular solo music (where he is more often highly successful) he frequently adopts realistic devices of a quaintly innocent kind, for lack of resources to utter otherwise his expressive intentions.[6]

GUSTAV HOLST

(1874–1934)

The English composer Gustav Holst did more than almost
any conductor or composer during the early years of the
twentieth century to perform Purcell's operas, presenting *Dio-
clesion*, *King Arthur* and *The Fairy-Queen* while musical director of Morley College. His appreciation was expressed in
'Henry Purcell: the dramatic composer of England
(1659–1695)'.

'Save me from my friends – I can protect myself from my enemies'.
HENRY PURCELL, more than anyone, would have been justified in
saying this. He has had kinder enemies than any other artist; for they
have only ignored him. In fact, he suffered and suffers still, as a composer, from a lack of *critical* appreciation.

To quote examples of uncritical appreciation, some writers have implied
that he was the most important of the Tudor composers, and on the other
hand he has been called 'the greatest English imitator of Handel'. He
was born about 1658, fifty-five years after Queen Elizabeth's death, and
died in 1695, when Handel was ten years of age.

He is generally considered to be England's greatest composer, owing
partly to the large amount of music he wrote in his short life, and partly
to its variety. This variety is, indeed, noteworthy. Purcell wrote chamber
music, church music, and dramatic music. Amongst his chamber music
we must include, together with his sonatas, a number of short sacred
vocal works, such as the two Evening Hymns. These have real beauty
and are far more important musically than his better-known services and
anthems which he wrote for Westminster Abbey, where he was organist
from 1680 until his death. To judge Purcell by these longer sacred works
would be as unfair as to judge Mozart by his Masses. Yet it is by his
church music that Purcell is known to most of his countrymen . . .

It is surely unnecessary nowadays to dwell on Purcell's gift of melody.
According to some it is excelled only by Mozart's . . . In addition to his
gift of melody there are his sense of harmony, his feeling for orchestral
colour, his humour, his intensity, his lyrical power . . . Yet all these
details of composition were subordinate to his amazing power of dramatic
characterisation.

This power has been possessed by very few opera composers. Indeed, many do not seem to have been aware of the necessity of cultivating it. They have thought it more important to study the idiosyncrasies of the particular opera singers engaged for a production than to consider the dramatic foundation on which to build the music. Musical characterisation is usually looked upon as a modern factor in opera. One instinctively thinks of Wagner. Both Purcell and Wagner used all their gifts of melody and harmony, all their mastery of orchestral colour, to give life to their characters and situations. But while Wagner painted huge scenes, each consistent in itself and at the same time part of a vaster whole, Purcell was content to paint little cabinet pictures.

But in one way Purcell is a finer stage composer than Wagner: his music is full of movement – of dance. His is the easiest music in all the world to act. Only those can realise fully the truth of this who have experienced the joy of moving to Purcell's music, whether in the ballroom or on the stage or in the garden; but especially in the garden.[7]

PETER WARLOCK
(1894–1930)

An inventive and sensitive composer, the Englishman Peter Warlock was renowned chiefly for his songs. In his short career – his death in 1930 appears to have been suicide – he established himself as an authority on Elizabethan music. Under his original name, Philip Heseltine, he edited early English music, including a volume of Purcell's fantasias for Curwen. Warlock also wrote about them in an article in the *Sackbut* in 1927.

Not long ago a distinguished British composer referred, in print, to 'the Elizabethan era which gave to the world the music of Purcell', and an intelligent German musician, on hearing a performance of one of the Fantasias for strings, detected in it the influence of Johann Sebastian Bach. A brief note on Purcell's orientation in musical history may not, therefore, be as superfluous as it should be if England gave more honour to her great musicians. Queen Elizabeth had been in her grave for more than half a century when Purcell was born, and these Fantasias were written five years before Bach first saw the light. Purcell was then in his twenty-third year. Among his middle-aged contemporaries were Pepys, Dryden, and Sir Isaac Newton. The aged author of *Religio Medici* had yet two years to live; Swift was a lad of thirteen; Congreve and Defoe mere children. It was in this year (1680) that Purcell succeeded his former master, Dr. John Blow, as organist of Westminster Abbey. As the greater part of Purcell's music with which the public is already familiar dates from the last twelve years of his life (1683–95), these Fantasias must be accounted early works. But Purcell matured early, and although these works were not deemed worthy of publication during his life-time (they have never appeared in print at all, for that matter, until the present year), they are immeasurably superior to the two sets of Sonatas which were published in 1683 and 1697 respectively and have been reprinted in modern times. Despite their startling originality, the Fantasias are essentially in the tradition of the Elizabethan polyphonists. They are the last heirs of the sixteenth century rather than the ancestors of the eighteenth. They stand at the end of a great period of English instrumental music, the crowning glory of a century and a half of rapid and continuous development . . .

Many who hear or read these Fantasias of Purcell for the first time will doubtless find them 'modern', in the sense of being in advance of their age; and assuredly we must go forward to Bach before we can find any music which displays such consummate mastery of all the devices of counterpoint allied to so wide a range of profoundly expressive harmony. Not that Purcell is to be regarded as a mere pioneer or anticipator whose promise others should fulfil: his achievements are positive and complete, and, despite his youth, he found – in these very works – his own fulfilment. He is a Janus-like figure in the history of music, looking backward into the past and forward into the future. But paradoxically enough it is in these early Fantasias, modelled on the old English tradition that was already considered *vieux jeu* in his own time, that he shows his greatest originality and finest musicianship, though the Sonatas, composed three years later, in which, he tells us, 'he has faithfully endeavoured a just imitation of the most famed Italian masters' no doubt seemed to his contemporaries far more 'modern' and up to date; indeed, it seems probable that Purcell could find neither publisher nor public for his Fantasias, and so turned to the more fashionable form of composition, for two violins and a figured bass.

The word 'modern' as applied to music has no æsthetic significance, and its use is somewhat pernicious; musical history is continually showing us how flimsy and unessential are the bases on which 'modernity' rests. In the early years of the seventeenth century there was much talk of the 'New Music', by which was meant the declamatory style evolved by those Italian composers, such as Peri and Caccini, who were experimenting with the musical drama. But to our ears to-day this so-called 'New Music' sounds completely stale and flat, while Dowland, whom the disciples of novelty rated old-fashioned, amazes us with the bold originality of his conceptions.

The quality of his music reveals Purcell as a man of genius far above his age: the forms in which it was cast were for the most part dictated by his age, and it is the unsatisfactory character of these forms that is largely responsible for the neglect of his music in this country and elsewhere. In the Fantasias, however, there is a perfect relation between form and content, and there can be little doubt that within a short time these works will be generally recognized as one of England's most significant contributions to the world's great music.[8]

PERCY GRAINGER
(1882–1961)

An immediate beneficiary of Warlock's activities was the Australian composer Percy Grainger. Grainger's interests in song and folksong were not dissimilar to Warlock's, though there was nothing of the antiquarian about the older composer. Warlock's edition of the fantasias was used by Grainger to illustrate a vibrant letter to the Canadian pianist and composer Maurice Lowe (b. 1902), then living in British Columbia. The letter, written in 1929 and headed simply 'in the train', discusses the benefits – and limitations – of the piano.

I delight to try to answer yr letter because the subject interests me especially, yr case being a particularly vital one, i.e., the case of the talented unconventional minded music lover who reaches music thru the piano and has the limitations of his approach. What is the great boon of the piano? That it opens the world of harmony and the possibility of florid arabesques as hardly any other instrument can. But it also tends to make our musical thought small (limited to 4 bar phrases, all phrases beginning and ending *together*). It gives us little insight into the very root of harmony and free musical form – different voices of different lengths and rhythms, beginning and ending at different moments, which interweave and together form harmony and formal impulses, such as

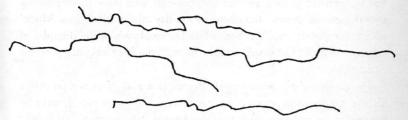

Should not the outlines of musical voices, in their normal condition, resemble the outlines of mountain ranges, each independent and individualistic in itself, but together forming block effects of majestic complexity?

The disgusting simplicity of modern life has laid itself like a disease over a great deal of music. What is the victory of modern civilization (over the Orient, for instance)? The victory of a deadening simplicity over a healthy complexity.

Of course not all our art is simple. Much of it forms *a corrective* to the weaknesses of our civilization, and it is these corrective examples we should study (among other things, of course), in my opinion.

Can you get a second piano (no matter how small and poor-toned) in your house? If so, all is very simple.

Take *Purcell's 'Three part, 4 part and 5 part Fantasias for Strings,'* recently edited by Peter Warlock, Curwen Edition. Order the score and 1 each of the string parts. Have these string parts played on your 2 pianos (violin I and viola on the 1st piano, and violin II and 'cello on 2nd piano), or, on four strings, if you have them. Or, yourself play 2 parts on 1 piano and have 2 other pianists play the other 2 parts on the other piano. Listen to the interplay of parts. Hear how they begin and end. Try experiments with them dynamically – see which expression marks are the most effective. See how these parts *breathe independently*, how each has a separate life, and thus is able to weave into a complex whole. I know of no lovelier examples of *real* many-voiced music (nor of British-mooded music) than these Purcells.[9]

IGOR STRAVINSKY
(1882–1971)

The Russian composer Igor Stravinsky was a lover of old English music and mentions Purcell on several occasions and in different contexts. He was once promised a complete set of the works of Purcell by the eccentric Lord Berners of Buscot Park, but seems never to have received it. (If Berners's mood was pink, an entirely pink luncheon might be served while pink pigeons flew overhead; from France Vera Stravinsky used to send him saffron dye for the pigeons and a blue powder for making blue mayonnaise.) In answer to Robert Craft's question 'You often associate "pathos" with chromaticism. Do you really believe in an innate connection?', in the chapter 'Some Musical Questions' of *Memories and Commentaries*, Stravinsky replied:

Of course not; the association is entirely due to conventions, like those of *musica riservata*; artists believe not in innate qualities but in art. Nevertheless, 'chromatic' and 'pathos' are connected, and the first musical use of chromatic, in the *misura cromatica*, was meant to indicate a rhythmic change for expressive, i.e. pathetic, purposes. I prefer to use chromatic in a limited sense, and in relation to diatonic. But we have acquired the habit of looking for *our* (post-Wagnerian) chromaticism in old music, with the result that contexts are grossly distorted. For example, in his setting of the funeral sentence *In the midst of Life we are in Death*, at the words 'Art justly displeased,' Purcell avoids the conventional cadence and composes one that was certainly intended, in one sense, to displease his audience; but the cadence pleases *us* in another sense, far more than the conventional one would have done.[10]

CONSTANT LAMBERT
(1905–51)

Constant Lambert, conductor and composer, was known for his lifelong appreciation of Purcell's music. He used it to create two ballets – *The Birthday of Oberon* and *Comus* – for Sadler's Wells, and conducted the 1946 production of *The*

Fairy-Queen which opened Covent Garden as a national home
for opera after the war. His love of Purcell's music, however,
did not prevent him from discussing it critically within the
context of musical thought of the 1930s, as these two extracts
from *Music Ho! a study of music in decline* attest.

Classical music has little sense of horror about it, not because classical
composers despised such an appeal to the nerves, but because they were
unable to achieve it. Dido's lament remains as deeply moving today as
when it was written – we have to make no mental adjustments to the
period in order to appreciate its emotional appeal; but *The Echo Dance of
the Furies* in the same opera can only be appreciated as a hieroglyphic of
the sinister – it makes no direct nervous physical appeal as does the other
music in the opera. On certain occasions Purcell, the most picturesque of
the pre-Romantic composers, could obtain an effect of strangeness and
awe as in the amazing passage which accompanies the words 'From your
sleepy mansion rise' in *The Indian Queen*; but for the most part his flexible
technique enabled him to express anything but the outré.[11]

And on Purcell's nationalism:

Dowland could absorb as much Italian influence as he wished without any
fear of losing his own unconsciously English personality.

Similarly, in a later period, when music was already beginning to show
the formal and cosmopolitan imprint of aristocratic tastes, Purcell was
able to graft the Italian manner on to his early post-Elizabethan manner
with no loss of national individuality. The happy and homogeneous duality
of his style is indeed symbolized by *Dido and Aeneas* where the exquisite
classicism of the Italianate court scenes is set against the rowdy nationalism
of the sailors' stews. Such a scene as the drunken sailors' chorus in *Dido*
would have been considered in the eighteenth century not only barbarously
national but intolerably vulgar. We get similar scenes in *The Beggar's
Opera*, it is true, but only as a burlesque which forms the most powerful
comment possible on the artificial taste of the time, for such a burlesque
would have been impossible in Purcell's day when mythological goddesses,
woodnymphs, dairymaids and ladies of the street met on equal terms.[12]

ELISABETH LUTYENS
(1906–83)

Elisabeth Lutyens, daughter of the architect Sir Edwin Lutyens, had begun studying music seriously at the École Normale in Paris in 1922. Her compositional activities during the 1930s appear to have been carried on in isolation from Continental developments, and her discovery of the Purcell fantasias, described below, resulted in a personal brand of serialism which found its first mature expression in the Chamber Concerto No. 1 of 1939.

It was Anne Macnaghten who [in the early 1930s] introduced me to André Mangeot, brother of the Director of the Paris École Normale I had briefly attended, for he had been coaching her quartet. He was a founder and leader of the International String Quartet and his rediscovery, editing and performances of the Purcell Fantasias (little known then) had a profound and lasting effect on me. It was hearing these works, with their equality of part-writing, coupled with my satiety – to screaming point – with diatonic cadential harmony, that led me to discover gradually, for my own compositional needs, what some years later I heard described as 'twelve-tone', 'serial' composition. I had not, as yet, heard the names, still less the music, of the new Viennese School.[13]

FRANCIS POULENC
(1899–1963)

For many years the accessibility of music of the French composer Francis Poulenc militated against his being considered a serious composer. By the time he attended the Aldeburgh Festival in 1956, though, his opera *Les Mamelles de Tirésias* had achieved brilliant success, and his position was such that his visit was partly to give a talk on his own musical style, 'Propos à batons rompus sur la musique'. Benjamin Britten's love of Purcell may have prompted Poulenc to consult him as to the identity of a tune he had heard, 'What a sad fate is mine.'

Hotel Splendide, Evian, 4 July [1956]
Cher Ben,

I want to tell you once again what joy it gave me to be with you at your exquisite Aldeburgh Festival. It is all so much *you* – full of intelligence, finesse, and heart. And from your window, I 'saw' Peter Grimes; and in London, I bought the fascinating records of *The Turn of the Screw*. All this has drawn me even closer to you, for whom I have so much love and admiration. Thank you.

The other day I heard an air by Purcell that moved me to tears. It is a passacaglia sung by an alto voice. The continuo on the cello goes something like this:

If you recognize it, can you tell me exactly what it is so that I can buy it. I embrace you, and Peter, too.

Francis[14]

BENJAMIN BRITTEN
(1913–76)

The recipient of Poulenc's letter, the English composer Benjamin Britten, had for many years claimed Purcell as an inspiration. His discovery of the music of *The Fairy-Queen* in the 1940s led to a still-born proposal to re-orchestrate the work, and he contributed to the collection of essays on Purcell's music which appeared in 1959; he also realized some of Purcell's songs and edited *Dido and Aeneas*. Of course, both composers were mentioned in the same breath by many critics, and Britten in fact invited such comparisons.

[*Billy Budd*] has a perfection of its own, and there is about this music and this perfection a touch of precariousness that never impairs its quality

– that touch of strangeness that Britten so rightly ascribes to his beloved Purcell.[15]

> Britten was to become known for his performing versions of Purcell's music. These were not always well received and had the character of realizations rather than editions, as the following note by Pears and himself makes clear.

This edition of Purcell's music which will eventually, it is hoped, include most of the songs from the Orpheus Britannicus and the Harmonia Sacra, as well as much of the chamber music, choral and orchestral music, is not intended to be a definitive edition or a work of reference. It is a performing edition for contemporary conditions.

Many of the pieces to be published have not been printed for 100 years, others are only available today in the admirable but expensive folios of the Purcell Society. Many more are published in all sorts of arrangements which do not seem to us to contain much of the Purcellian spirit. This edition is not the work of musicologists and therefore the solution of problems such as ornamentation has not been attempted. Most singers today are either unwilling or unable to perform the 'Graces' – which Purcell may have expected and we have therefore only printed the notes which Purcell himself printed. Those singers who wish to 'grace' the songs will do so at their own pleasure.

It is clear that the figured basses in Purcell's day were realised in a manner personal to the player. In this edition the basses have also, inevitably, been realised in a personal way. But it has been the constant endeavour of the arranger to apply to these realisations something of that mixture of clarity, brilliance, tenderness and strangeness which shines out in all Purcell's music.[16]

> Britten's views, however, are best summed up in his interview with Murray Schafer from the early 1960s.

SCHAFER: As the editor of Purcell's music do you think there are any aspects of Purcell's achievement which have not been fully appreciated?

BRITTEN: Purcell is not fully appreciated in this country. *Dido and Aeneas* is unquestionably a masterpiece, but it is not a box-office success and therefore it is only rarely performed. It's the same old business of the inveterate philistinism of this country. They want us to perform Purcell in Sweden.

SCHAFER: Are there any aspects of Purcell's achievement which have
interested you in particular?

BRITTEN: Purcell is a great master at handling the English language
in song, and I learned much from him. I recall a critic
once asking me from whom I had learned to set English
poetry to music. I told him Purcell; he was amazed. I
suppose he expected me to say folk music and Vaughan
Williams.

SCHAFER: Writing in 1952 Peter Pears referred to your *First Canticle*
as your finest vocal piece to date. Would you have agreed
with him at that time?

BRITTEN: Yes, I think so. The *First Canticle* was a new invention in
a sense although it was certainly modelled on the Purcell
Divine Hymns; but few people knew their Purcell well
enough to realize that. [17]

MICHAEL TIPPETT
(b. 1905)

Like Britten, the English composer Michael Tippett was
attracted to Purcell as a distinctive voice, and as a composer
whom he felt had been neglected nationally both in the concert
halls and in musical education.

Holst and Vaughan Williams, and other composers of their generation,
were very drawn towards folksong and the music of the Elizabethans.
But it was my generation, including, of course, Britten, that found a new
source of inspiration and a fresh example in Purcell.

We were not taught Purcell in the Conservatoire: we discovered him
independently for ourselves. When I went to study at the Royal College
of Music in London in the early twenties, Purcell's music was much less
played than it is these days. It seems to me incomprehensible now that
his work was not even recommended in composition lessons as a basic
study for the setting of English. I may have been unlucky, but I think
the omission was general. However, when I was nineteen, I began to
conduct small amateur choirs with the object of studying in action, as it
were, the English madrigal school – a repertory equally neglected in my

Royal College training. Thus, when much later I found out about Purcell, I already had a good ear for the setting of English by his immediate predecessors. Byrd, Tallis, Gibbons, Dowland were no longer names in a history book, but composers of living music. Through their works, these composers were as alive to me as their great contemporaries, Shakespeare, Marlowe, Spencer and Sidney.

I think it is fairly true to say that the English worship of Handel, and later of Mendelssohn, effectively nullified any possible influence of Purcell. His scores were unavailable, lost from the public gaze, and his music almost unperformed. The Elizabethan composers were also unheard, just as English folksong was unrecorded. But at the turn of the century, Elizabethan madrigals and Tudor church music were rediscovered and printed, the unmatched riches of folksong collected, and the Purcell Society itself was founded, for the publication of that composer's works in *urtext* editions.

The personal discovery of Purcell which Britten and I made later led us not only to initiate performances of as much music as possible, but also to issue performing editions through our respective publishers. Eventually, too, we produced recordings of Purcell's music. Altogether, these have demonstrated that Purcell is a European voice, a master in his own unique right.[18]

PETER MAXWELL DAVIES

(b. 1934)

Peter Maxwell Davies also found himself stimulated and inspired by Purcell's music. His career has not been without controversy, and his music theatre pieces of the late 1960s and 1970s remain undimmed by the passing of time. Davies is clear that his approach to Purcell has been one of realization and arrangement. As his note on his arrangements of Purcell's fantasia and two pavans attests, there is no pretence of authenticity.

I have long been fascinated by Purcell's music, but utterly bored by well-meaning 'authentic' performances, which possibly get every double-dotted rhythm right but convey no sense of Purcell's intensity of feeling, sense of fun or sheer outrageousness. I feel the profoundest respect for the 'great' composers of the past, but have no feeling of slavish reverence towards them whatever – after all, they were living, real people, not priests. Already in the early Sixties I *used* Monteverdi's Vespers in original compositions and, as a preparatory stage in the composition process, reworked several great chunks of that work for the choir and orchestra of Cirencester Grammar School, where I was teaching – and I suspect that, paradoxically, I came a great deal nearer to the sound and spirit of the original, with an orchestration including clarinets and valve-trumpets, than many a 'pure' version, discreetly and beautifully performed. Musical purity in these matters is about as interesting as moral purity. I am sure that many people will consider my Purcell realizations wholly immoral.

In *Missa Super l'Homme Armé* I subjected an incomplete anonymous fifteenth-century Agnus Dei to a sequence of transformations which parodied many styles from different periods including in the score a special 78 r.p.m. recording of an eighteenth-century chamber organ, played on a pre-electric horn gramophone. This same chamber organ, in my cottage in Dorset, with its brazen twelfth stop, determined the character of my realization of the Purcell Fantasia on a Ground, in which the bass clarinet holds the ground bass throughout. This same horn gramophone influenced the realisations of the two pavans, for I have a collection of foxtrot records from the Twenties and Thirties, and my treatment of the Purcell dances was sparked off by these. They were very much preparatory studies for a large orchestral work, *St Thomas Wake*.[19]

Notes

The sources quoted in this book range from seventeenth-century writings to modern-day editions, and this, together with the desire to preserve as much of the character of the contemporary sources as possible so that the reader could see them as Purcell did, militated against a consistent editorial policy.
Generally, the version quoted of any printed text – poem, dedication, prologue and so on – is the first edition, and is the source listed below. Quotations from manuscript sources, many of which were checked against the originals, are taken from the cited transcriptions. Spelling corrections have largely been eschewed, original capitalization and italicization have been retained except where otherwise indicated and square brackets have been used sparingly.

I Early life and the Chapel Royal

1. Samuel Pepys, *The Diary of Samuel Pepys*, ed. R. C. Latham and W. Matthews, I (London, 1970), p. 63: 21 February 1660.
2. Ibid., pp. 265–6: 14 October 1660.
3. Ibid., II (London, 1970), p. 41: 23 February 1661.
4. Ibid., VIII (London, 1974), p. 59: 13 February 1667.
5. Lord Chamberlains Papers, 5/52, p. 106: 17 September 1661, quoted in David Baldwin, *The Chapel Royal, Ancient and Modern* (London, 1990), p. 191.
6. Lord Chamberlains Papers, 5/137, p. 292: 20 August 1663, quoted in Andrew Ashbee, *Records of English Court Music*, I (Snodland, Kent, 1986), pp. 47–8.
7. Pepys, *Diary*, VI (London, 1972), p. 93: 30 April 1665.
8. Ibid., pp. 132–3: 20 June 1665.
9. Ibid., p. 192: 15 August 1665.
10. Ibid., VII (London, 1972), pp. 376–7: 20 November 1666.
11. Ibid., p. 274: 4 September 1666.
12. Ibid., pp. 274–5.
13. Ibid., p. 271: 2 September 1666.
14. Ibid., p. 381: 23 November 1666.
15. Ibid.
16. John Playford, Publisher's Note, in *Catch that Catch Can, or The Musical Companion* (London, 1667).

17. Pepys, *Diary*, IV (London, 1971), pp. 393–4: 22 November 1663.
18. Ibid., VIII, p. 515: 1 November 1667.
19. Ibid., pp. 529–30: 15 November 1667.
20. Ibid., IV, p. 120: 1 May 1663.
21. Ibid., VIII, p. 73: 20 February 1667.
22. 'Nell Gwynne' (1669), in *Poems on Affairs of State*, I, ed. George de F. Lord (New Haven, 1963), p. 420. It survives in manuscript in *GB-Lbl* Harleian MS 7317.

II Singers, singing and a celebration of music

1. Lord Chamberlains Papers, 5/140, p. 384: 17 December 1673, quoted in Franklin B. Zimmerman, *Henry Purcell 1659–1695: his life and times* (Philadelphia, 2/1983), p. 291.
2. Lord Chamberlains Papers, 2 February 1674, quoted in H. C. De Lafontaine, *The King's Musick* (London, 1909), p. 265.
3. Lord Chamberlains Papers, 5/140, p. 384: 17 December 1673, quoted in De Lafontaine, *The King's Musick*, p. 263.
4. Lord Chamberlains Papers, 5/140, p. 309: 10 June 1673, quoted in Ashbee, *English Court Music*, p. 126.
5. Lord Chamberlains Papers, 5/138, pp. 96–7: 6 November 1663, quoted in Ashbee, *English Court Music*, p. 49.
6. Matthew Locke to Henry Purcell, ?c. 1676, transcribed by E. F. Rimbault and quoted in William Cummings, *Purcell* (London, 1881), p. 27.
7. John Hawkins, *A General History of the Science and Practice of Music* (London, 1853), II, p. 693.
8. Aphra Behn, 'On hearing Mr. P. sing', in *Miscellany* (London, 1685), pp. 216–18. Maureen Duffy, in *The Passionate Shepherdess: Aphra Behn 1640–89* (London, 2/1989), pp. 142, 307 n. 5, suggests with no foundation that Daniel Purcell is the 'Mr P.' intended here.
9. Samuel Taylor Coleridge, 'To W. L. Esq. while he sang a song to Purcell's music', Sonnet XII in *The Annual Anthology* (London, 1800), II p. 156. The extant manuscript bears the date 14 September 1797; see *The Complete Poetical Works of Samuel Taylor Coleridge*, ed. Ernest Hartley Cleridge (Oxford, 1912), I, p. 236.
10. Pierre Motteux, *Gentleman's Journal*, January 1692, pp. 4–5.
11. Henry Purcell, Dedication, *Welcome to all the Pleasures* (London, 1684).
12. Motteux, *Gentleman's Journal*, November 1692, p. 18.
13. Anthony Aston, *A Brief Supplement to Colley Cibber . . .* (London, c. 1747), p. 18.
14. Christopher Smart, *Ode for Musick on St Cecilia's Day*, pt. 8; first published

in Robert Dodsley, *Museum*, 13 September 1746, I, pp. 496–8, as 'Warlike Music, and Church Music. The two last stanzas of Mr Smart's Ode on St Cecilia's Day'.

15. John Playford, Dedication, in *Catch that Catch Can*.
16. John Playford, Advertisement relating to the First Book, in *Catch that Catch Can* (London, 2/1673).
17. Henry Playford, Preface, in *The Pleasant Musical Companion* (London, 5/1707).
18. Henry Purcell, 'Young John the Gard'ner' (1683), in *Musical Companion*, no. 35.
19. Henry Purcell, 'Song with Music on the 7 Bishops' (1689), in *Musical Companion*, no. 20.
20. John Lenton, A Rebus on Mr. *Hen Purcell's* name, in *Musical Companion*, no. 73. The text was by Mr Tomlinson.
21. Henry Purcell, 'A Song in Commendation of the Viol' (1693), in *Musical Companion*, no. 50.
22 Hawkins, *A General History*, II, p. 747.
23. Ibid.
24. ?Henry Purcell, 'Tom the Taylor', in *Musical Companion*, no. 110; ascribed to Henry Hall in the 5th edition, but to Purcell in editions both before and after.
25. ?Purcell, 'Tom the Taylor', in *The Works of Henry Purcell*, XXII (London, 1922), p. xxi; text rewritten and revised by W. Barclay Squire.
26. Middlesex County Records, Sacrament Certificate 4/13, quoted in Zimmerman, *Henry Purcell*, pp. 95–6.

III The *Sonnata's of III Parts* and a battle for an organ

1. Roger North, *Roger North on Music*, ed. John Wilson (London, 1959), p. 307 n. 57, written *c.* 1695, and p. 310 n. 65, written 1710–20.
2. Ibid., p. 307, written *c.* 1725.
3. Ibid., pp. 307, 309–11, written *c.* 1725.
4. Pepys, *Diary*, IV, p. 428: 21 December 1663.
5. Ibid., VIII, pp. 54, 56–7: 12 February 1667.
6. Anonymous passage quoted by John Playford in *An Introduction to the Skill of Musick* (London, 11/1687), p. 34.
7. Ibid., pp. 34–5.
8. Ibid., p. 46.
9. Ibid., pp. 46–7.
10. John Macky, *A Journey through England in Familiar Letters* (London, 1714), I, p. 110.

11. *London Gazette*, 28–31 May 1683, p. 2.
12. Ibid., 7–11 June 1683, p. 2.
13. Ibid., 1–5 November 1683, p. 2, and in other numbers.
14. Henry Purcell, Dedication, *Sonnata's of III Parts* (London, 1683); the first impression opens with 'May it please yo[r] Maj[ty]' and does not have the second 'most' in the valediction: see Henry Purcell, *Twelve Sonatas of Three Parts*. ed. Michael Tilmouth, in *The Works of Henry Purcell*. 5 (1976), p. x.
15. Henry Purcell, Preface, *Sonnata's of III Parts*.
16. Roger North, *The Life of the Right Hon. Francis North, Baron Guilford*; unpublished material for North's biography quoted in North, *North on Music*, p. 47.
17. Roger North, *Cursory Notes of Musick (c. 1698–c. 1703): A Physical, Psychological and Critical Theory*, ed. Mary Chan and J. C. Kassler (Kensington, Australia, 1986), p. 229.
18. Vestry Minutes of St Katherine Cree 1686/7, *GB-Lgc* MS 1196/1, quoted in Zimmerman, *Henry Purcell*, pp. 292–3. The case of the organ Purcell played is still extant; see James Boeringer, *Organa Britannica*, II (New Jersey, 1986), pp. 180–81.
19. Minutes of St Katherine Cree, quoted in Zimmerman, *Henry Purcell*, pp. 134–5.
20. Roger North, 'The Musicall Grammarian', in *North on Music*, p. 354, written *c.* 1726.
21. Ibid.
22. Thomas Tudway to his son, transcribed and edited by Percy A. Scholes in 'Henry Purcell: a sketch of a busy life', *Musical Quarterly*, ii (1916), pp. 451–2.

IV Two coronations and a revolution

1. John Evelyn, *The Diary of John Evelyn*, ed. E. S. de Beer (Oxford, 1955), IV, pp. 413–14: 6 February 1685. Material in square brackets has been drawn from other sources, and angle brackets are used to indicate editorial insertions; for further explanation of de Beer's editorial method see vol. I.
2. Ibid., p. 419: 5 March 1685.
3. Ibid., pp. 437–8: 23 April 1685.
4. Francis Sandford, *The History of the Coronation of . . . James II . . .* (London, 1687), pp. 29–30.
5. Ibid., p. 70–1.
6. *GB-Ob* Rawl. MS.D., 872, p. 124; as quoted in Zimmerman, *Henry Purcell*, p. 125.
7. Sandford, *History*, p. 82.

8. Ibid., p. 102.

9. Ibid., p. 104.

10. Ibid., p. 107.

11. Lord Chamberlain Papers, 5/147, p. 213; 9 November 1686, quoted in Ashbee, *English Court Music* (1987), II, p. 12.

12. Evelyn, *Diary*, IV, pp. 534–5: 29 December 1686.

13. Ibid., p. 537: 30 January 1687.

14. Ibid., p. 547: 19 April 1687.

15. Ibid., pp. 610–11: 13, 16, 17 December 1688.

16. Ibid., pp. 611–12: 18 December 1688.

17. *London Gazette*, 11–15 April 1689, p. 1.

18. Evelyn, *Diary*, IV, pp. 632–3: 11 April 1689.

19. Hawkins, *A General History*, II, p. 743–4.

V Publishing, pedagogy and a passing

1. Henry Playford, Dedication, in *Harmonia Sacra*, bk I (London, 1688).

2. Henry Playford, 'To the Reader', in *Harmonia Sacra*, bk I.

3. Henry Playford, Dedication, in *Harmonia Sacra*, bk I (London, 2/1703).

4. Motteux, *Gentleman's Journal*, 1693, p. 3.

5. Henry Playford, Dedication, in *Harmonia Sacra*, bk II (London, 1693).

6. T. Brown, 'Long and dark Ignorance our Isle o'erspread', in *Harmonia Sacra*, bk II.

7. Henry Playford, Advertisement to the Reader, in *Deliciae Musicae*, bk I (London, 1695).

8. ?John Playford, 'This PLAYFORD'S Shadow doth present', in *A Brief Introduction to the Skill of Musick* (London, 3/1660).

9. John Playford, Preface, ibid.

10. Henry Purcell, in *An Introduction to the Skill of Musick* (London, 12/1694), p. 144.

11. Ibid.

12. Edward Phillips, *The New World of Words* (London, 5/1696); there is doubt about Purcell's exact contribution to this project: see Graham Strahle, *Purcell: contributor of musical terms to* The New World of Words *or not?*, paper given at the conference 'Performing the Music of Henry Purcell', Exeter College, Oxford, 1993.

13. Frances Purcell, Dedication, in Henry Purcell, *Choice Lessons for the Harpsichord or Spinet* (London, 1696).

14. Henry Purcell, Opening Instructions, *Choice Lessons*.

15. Charles Burney, *A General History of Music*, III (London, 1789), p. 559.

16. Henry Purcell to the Dean of Exeter, 2 November 1686, MS in *GB-EXc*, quoted in Zimmerman, *Henry Purcell*, p. 136.

17. Hawkins, *A General History*, II, p. 564n.

18. Charles Sedley, verse two of 'The Royal Knotter', in *The Poetical Works of Charles Sedley* (London, 1707), pp. 146.

19. William Shakespeare, *The Tragedy of Othello*, in *The Riverside Shakespeare*, ed. G. Blakemore Evans (Boston, 1974), IV. ii. 59–62.

20. 'Ode on the Death of the Queen', in *Poems on Affairs of State*, III (London, 1704), pp. 360–61. For the tortuous history of this text see the modern edition of the collection, V, ed. William J. Cameron (New Haven, 1971), pp. 444–6.

21. Narcissus Luttrell, *A Brief Historical Relation of State Affairs from Sept. 1678 to April 1714* (Oxford, 1857), III, p. 416: 22 December 1694.

22. Ibid., p. 417: 25 December 1694.

23. Ibid., p. 418: 27 December 1694.

24. Ibid., p. 418: 29 December 1694.

25. Ibid., pp. 418–9: 29 December 1694.

26. Ibid., pp. 420–21: 3 January 1695.

27. Ibid., p. 442: 21 February 1695.

28. Henry Howard, Duke of Norfolk, *The Form and Proceeding to the Funeral of her late Majesty Queen Mary II* (London, 1695), p. 4.

29. Thomas Tudway, *GB-Lbl* Harleian MS, iv, Introduction.

VI Purcell on the stage

1. Mrs A. Buck to Mary Clarke, transcribed by Mark Goldie in 'The Earliest Notice of Purcell's *Dido and Aeneas*', *Early Music*, xx (1992), p. 393.

2. Thomas D'Urfey, 'Epilogue to the Opera of *Dido and Aeneas*', in *New Poems* (London, 1689), pp. 82–3. The table of contents refers to 'Mrs Priests' boarding-school.

3. George Bernard Shaw, 'Music at Bow', *Star*, 21 February 1889, quoted in *Shaw's Music*, ed. Dan H. Laurence (London, 1981), I, pp. 559–60.

4. Gustav Holst, 'Musick', *Athenaeum*, 23 November 1895, p. 725.

5. Charles Reid, *Thomas Beecham: an independent biography* (London, 1961), pp. 177–8.

6. Roger Savage, unpublished prologue to *Dido and Aeneas* (1989, rev. 1994). The 1989 production, conducted by Gary Cooper, included Margaret Laurie's reconstruction of the all-sung prologue. Savage's spoken prologue celebrated the tenth anniversary of the admission of women to New College, Oxford.

7. Motteux, *Gentleman's Journal*, January 1692, p. 36.

8. John Dryden, From the Epistle Dedicatory, *Amphitryon* (London, 1690).

9. North, *North on Music*, pp. 353–4, written *c.* 1726.

10. John Downes, *Roscius Anglicanus*, ed. Judith Milhous and Robert D. Hume (London, 1987), p. 89.

11. *London Gazette*, 3–7 July 1690, p. 2.

12. ?Henry Purcell, Advertisement, *The Vocal and Instrumental Musick of the Prophetess* . . . (London, 1691). The manuscript of this note is in *GB-Lbl* Stowe MS 755, fol. 35r.

13. John Dryden, published as if by Henry Purcell, epistle to *Dioclesian*, transcribed and edited by Roswell G. Ham as 'Dryden's Dedication for *The Music of the Prophetess*, 1691', Publications of the Modern Language Association, 1 (1935), pp. 1065–75. The manuscript is in *GB-Lbl* Stowe MS 755, fols. 34, 35v.

14. John Dryden, Prologue, *Dioclesian* (London, 1690).

15. *Muses Mercury*, January 1707, pp. 4–5.

16. John Dryden, Epistle Dedicatory, *King Arthur* (London, 1691).

17. North, *North on Music*, p. 217, written before 1701.

18. Ibid., p. 215, 216–7.

19. Thomas Gray to Horace Walpole, 3 January 1736, *The Correspondence of Gray, Walpole, West and Ashton 1734–1771*, ed. Paget Toynbee (Oxford, 1915), I, pp. 57–9.

20. Sylvia Townsend Warner, *The Diaries of Sylvia Townsend Warner*, ed. Claire Harman (London, 1994), pp. 13–4: 18 February 1928.

21. Motteux, *Gentleman's Journal*, January 1692, p. 5.

22. Preface, *The Fairy-Queen* (London, 1692).

23. *Fairy-Queen*, p. 40.

24. Motteux, *Gentleman's Journal*, May 1692, p. 26.

25. Roger North, *The Musicall Gramarian 1728*, ed. Mary Chan and Jamie Kassler (Cambridge, 1990), p. 201; North incorrectly places this scene in *King Arthur*.

26. *Flying Post*, 9–11 October 1701, p. 2.

27. Frances Purcell, Dedication, in Henry Purcell, *A Collection of Ayres Composed for the Theatre* (London, 1696).

28. *Muses Mercury*, January 1707, p. 10. The works that were 'now Preparing' included Thomas Clayton's *Rosamond*, John Eccles's *Semele* and Daniel Purcell's opera based in *Orlando Furioso* and his masque *Orpheus and Euridice*.

29. North, *Musicall Gramarian 1728*, p. 206.

30. Charles Gildon, *The Complete Art of Poetry* (London, 1718), I, p. 103.

31. Charles Gildon, *The Life of Thomas Betterton* (London, 1710), pp. 167–9.

32. Daniel Defoe, from 'A Proposal to prevent the exspensive importation of

Foreign musicians &c, by forming an Academy of our own', in *Augusta Triumphans* (London, 1728), p. 18.

33. George Dyson, *The Progress of Music* (London, 1932), pp. 116–17.

VII 'O mourn, ye sacred Muses, mourn'

1. Hawkins, *A General History*, II, p. 748.
2. Ibid., pp. 653–4.
3. Henry Purcell, Will, Public Record Office, PCC 243.
4. *Flying Post*, 23–6 November 1695, p. 2.
5. *Post Boy*, 26–8 November 1695, p. 1.
6. Text from Henry Purcell's tablet, Westminster Abbey.
7. Frances Purcell, Dedication, in Henry Purcell, *Ten Sonata's in Four Parts* (London, 1697).
8. Henry Playford, Note, in *An Introduction to the Skill of Musick* (London, 13/1697).
9. Frances Purcell, Dedication, in Henry Purcell, *Orpheus Britannicus*, bk I (London, 1698).
10. Henry Playford, 'The Bookseller to the Reader', in Purcell, *Orpheus Britannicus*, bk. I.
11. Henry Playford, Dedication, in Henry Purcell, *Orpheus Britannicus*, bk II (London, 1702).
12. Henry Playford, 'The Bookseller to the Reader', in Purcell, *Orpheus Britannicus*, bk II.
13. John Dryden, 'Ode on the Death of Mr Henry Purcell' in Purcell, *Orpheus Britannicus*, bk I.
14. John Sheffield, Duke of Buckingham, 'Ode on the Death of Henry Purcell', in *The Works of John Sheffield, Duke of Buckingham* (London, 1723), pp. 184–6.
15. Evelyn, *Diary*, V, p. 289: 30 May 1698.
16. George Granville, Baron Lansdowne, Epilogue, *The Jew of Venice* (London, 1701).

VIII From beyond the grave

1. Thomas Brown, *Letters from the Dead to the Living . . . the second part* (London, 2/1707), pp. 158–65.

IX 'The devine Purcell' – Purcell recalled

1. Thomas Tudway, *GB-Lbl* Harleian MS 7337–7342: 1714–1720.
2. *Universal Journal*, 25 July 1724, p. 3.

3. Oliver Goldsmith, from 'On the different Schools of Music', *British Magazine*, ed. T. B. Smollet and O. Goldsmith (London, 1760), p. 75.

4. Burney, *History of Music* III (London, 1789), pp. 485, 483, 506–9; misnumbered in edition.

5. Gerard Manley Hopkins, 'Henry Purcell', in *The Poems of Gerard Manley Hopkins*, ed. Robert Bridges (London, 1918), p. 42. The manuscript is dated Oxford, April 1879.

6. Gerard Manley Hopkins to Robert Bridges, 26 May 1879, *The Letters of Gerard Manley Hopkins to Robert Bridges*, ed. Claude Colleer Abbott (London, 1935), p. 83. For an explanation of the complex state of Hopkins's manuscripts see Norman H. Mackenzie, *The Poetical Works of Gerard Manley Hopkins* (Oxford, 1990), Introduction and pp. 402–4.

7. Hopkins to Bridges, 22 June 1879, *Letters*, p. 84.

8. Hopkins to Bridges, 4 January 1883, *Letters*, p. 170–71.

9. George Bernard Shaw, 'An English *Meistersinger*', *Star*, 2 May 1890, quoted in *Shaw's Music*, II, p. 55.

10. George Bernard Shaw, 'A Suppressed Notice of *Ivanhoe*', *World*, 4 February 1891, quoted in *Shaw's Music*, II, pp. 256–7.

11. George Bernard Shaw, 'English Music', *World*, 14 March 1894, quoted in *Shaw's Music*, III, p. 160.

12. Joseph Bennett, 'Henry Purcell: an appreciation', *Musical Times*, xxxvi (1895), pp. 725, 730.

13. JFF, 'Henry Purcell', *Illustrated London News*, 16 November 1895, p. 604. The author who hid behind the initials has yet to be identified.

14. ?J. S. Shedlock, Editorial, *Monthly Music Record*, xxv (1895), p. 300.

15. Donald Francis Tovey, 'The Main Stream of Music' (1938), in *Essays and Lectures on Music*, ed. Hubert J. Foss (London, 1949), pp. 336–7.

16. Donald Francis Tovey, 'Musical Textures', in *A Musician Talks* (London, 1941), pp. 12–13.

17. *Musical Britain 1951* (London, 1951), p. 139.

18. J. A. Westrup, 'Purcell's Reputation', *Musical Times*, c (1959), p. 318.

X Composers on Purcell – Purcell regain'd

1. Joseph Addison to William Congreve, August 1699, *William Congreve, Letters and Documents*, ed. John C. Hodges (London, 1964), p. 203.

2. R. J. S. Stevens (from Mr Savage in 1775), 'Anecdotes', *GB-Cpl* MS, fol. 18.

3. Henry Carey, from 'The Poet's Resentment', in *Poems on Several Occasions* (London, 1729), pp. 75–8.

4. William Boyce, *Cathedral Music*, II (London, 1768), p. ix.

5. John Stafford Smith, *A Collection of English Songs* (London, 1779), p. vii.

6. C. Hubert H. Parry, 'The Rise of Secular Music', in *The Art of Music* (London, 1893), pp. 162–3.

7. Gustav Holst, 'Henry Purcell: the dramatic composer of England (1658–1695)', in *The Heritage of Music*, ed. Hubert J. Foss (London, 1927), pp. 46–7, 51–2.

8. Peter Warlock, 'Purcell's Fantasias for Strings', *Sackbut*, vii (1927), pp. 281, 285.

9. Percy Aldridge Grainger to Maurice Lowe, *The All-Round Man: selected letters of Percy Grainger 1914–1961*, ed. Malcolm Gilles and David Pear (Oxford, 1994), pp. 100–102.

10. Igor Stravinsky and Robert Craft, *Memories and Commentaries* (London, 1960), pp. 115–16.

11. Constant Lambert, *Music Ho! a study of music in decline* (London, 1934), p. 62.

12. Ibid., pp. 129–30.

13. Elisabeth Lutyens, *A Goldfish Bowl* (London, 1972), pp. 68–9.

14. Francis Poulenc to Benjamin Britten, 4 July [1956], *Francis Poulenc 'Echo and Source': selected correspondence 1915–1963*, translated and edited by Sidney Buckland (London, 1991), pp. 240–41.

15. Fred Goldbeck, '*Billy Budd*: first impressions', *Opera*, iii (1952), p. 16.

16. Peter Pears and Benjamin Britten, *Seven Songs* [from *Orpheus Britannicus*] (London, 1946), Introduction.

17. Murray Schafer, *British Composers in Interview* (London, 1963), pp. 120–21.

18. Michael Tippett, *Music of the Angels*, ed. Meirion Bowen (London, 1980), pp. 67–8.

19. Peter Maxwell Davies, 'Purcell: fantasia and two pavans', programme note (1968), quoted in Paul Griffiths, *Peter Maxwell Davies* (London, 1982), pp. 146–7.

Index

Abel, John, 49
Academy of Ancient Music, 136
Alberici, Vincentio, 37
Aldeburgh Festival, 166–7
Aldrich, Henry, 62
Anglican Church, 27, 30–31
Anne, Queen, (earlier Princess of Denmark), 61, 75
anthems, 67
Aristotle, 106
Arne, Thomas, 141
Arts Council, 149
Ashwell, Mary, 10
Aston, Anthony, 22
Athenaeum, 82
Atkins, Samuel, 8

Baggs, Zachary, 103
Bannister, John, 10.
Baptista (Giovanni Battista Draghi), 37, 43–4
Bardock, Edward, 49
Barkhurst, Mr, 21
bawdiness, 27, 29–30
Bax, Ernest Belford, 81
Beach, Mr, 43
Beecham, Thomas, 83
Behn, Aphra, 18–19
Bennett, Joseph, 145–6
Bentham, Samuel, 49
Berners, Lord, 164
Bettenham, Thomas, 49
Betterton, Thomas, 86, 87, 91
Birkenshaw, John, 67
birthday odes, 22, 72
Blagrave, Thomas, 10, 50
Blow, John, 21, 26, 42–3, 44, 49, 50, 63, 114, 120, 127, 146, 161
Blunt, Charles, 21
Borrowdell, Giles, 31
Boucher, Josias, 49
Bowen, Jemmy, 22
Boyce, William, 140, 157

Breefe Introduction to the Skill of Musick, 65–6
Bridges, Robert, 142, 143
Bridgman, William, 22
Britten, Benjamin, 166–9, 170
Brouncker, Lord, 37
Brown, Richard, 29
Brown, Thomas, 63, 127–32
Buck, Mrs A., 79
Buckingham, Duke of, *see* Villiers, George
Buckingham and Normanby, 1st Duke of, *see* Sheffield, John
Burnet, Dr, 54
Burney, Charles, 69, 139–42
Butler, Charlotte, 97
Byrd, William, 148

Caccini, Giulio, 162
Caesar (Smegergill), William, 9
Carey, Henry, 156
Carissimi, Giacomo, 37, 62
Carr, John, 39, 40, 87
Carr, Robert, 21
Carteret, Sir Charles, 21
Castlemaine, Countess of, *see* Villiers, Barbara
catches, 24–30
Catch that Catch Can (or *The Musical Companion*), 8, 24–7
Catherine of Braganza (Queen Consort of Charles II), 11
Catholic Church, 12, 20, 27, 47–8, 51–3
Cato, 95
Cavendish, Lord Henry, 115
Cavendish, Mary, 115
Cavendish, Lady Rhoda, 71, 115–16
Cecil family, 20
Cecilia, St., 20–24
Chapel Royal, 4–5, 15, 17
Chapelin, John, 114
Charde, John, 49
Charles II, King, 3, 4, 9, 10–11, 12, 17, 40, 47, 93, 94, 148
Child, William, 49, 50

Purcell, Thomas, (Henry's father or uncle), 3
Purcell Society, 29, 147, 151, 170
Purcell's Head Tavern, 29

Rameau, Jean-Philippe, 138
Rebeck, Andrew, 49
A Rebus on Mr. *Hen Purcell's* Name, 28
religion
  Church of England, 27, 30–31
  Roman Catholicism, 12, 20, 27, 47–8, 51–3
Richardson, Thomas, 49
Richelieu, Cardinal, 101
ritornellos, 67
Rizzio, David, 138
Roger, John, 24
Rogers, Henry, 40
Roman Catholic Church, 12, 20, 27, 47–8, 51–3
Rootham, Cyril, 99
Roscius Anglicanus, 86–7
Roseingrave, Thomas, 44
Royal College of Music, 82, 83, 169

Sacheverell, Henry, 63
Sadler's Wells, 164
St. Anthony's fire, 74
St. Cecilia's Day celebrations, 20–24
Saint-Évremond, Charles de, 106–7
St. Katherine Cree, Church of, 42–3
Samuel, Thomas, 21
Sancroft, William, 27
Sandford, Francis, 48–51
Sandwich, 1st Earl of, *see* Mountagu, Edward
Saunderson, James, 21
Savage, Mr, 155
Savage, Roger, 83–5
Savile, George, Marquess of Halifax, 93–7, 118–19
Sayer, John, 49
Schafer, Murray, 168–9
Schütz, Heinrich, 149, 158
Scipione del Palla, 38
Scott, Walter, 115, 144
Sedley, Charles, 72
semi-operas, 79–85, 87–109
Settle, Elkanah, 16
Seymour, Charles, 6th Duke of Somerset, 88, 103–4
Shadwell, Thomas, 92

Shakespeare, William, 73, 87, 99, 106, 123, 136, 148
Shaw, George Bernard, 80–82, 144–5
Shedlock, J. S., 146
Sheffield, John, 1st Duke of Buckingham and Normanby, 3rd Earl of Mulgrave, 121–2
Showers, Mr, 21
Siface (Giovanni Francesco Grossi), 52
singing, 16–19, 22
  of catches, 24, 25–6
  ornamentation in, 22, 37–8, 69–70
  Purcell's style of, 18–19, 22
smallpox, 73–4
Smart, Christopher, 23–4
Smith, Fr Bernard, 42, 43–4
Smith, Henry, 49
Smith, John Stafford, 157–8
Snow, Mr, 43
Snow, Moses, 31
Somerset, 6th Duke of, *see* Seymour, Charles
'Song in Commendation of the Viol', 28
'Song with Music on the 7 Bishops', 27–8
Southerne, Thomas, 85
Southey, Robert, 19
Soutten, B., 82
spinets, 67–70
Spong, John, 3
Sprat, Dr, 55
Squire, W. Barclay, 29
Staggins, Nicholas, 22, 48, 49, 51
Stanford, Charles Villiers, 82–3
Stevens, R. J. S., 155
Stradella, Alessandro, 113
Stravinsky, Igor, 164
Stravinsky, Vera, 164
Sturgiss, Julian, 144
subscriptions, 39–40, 87–8
Sullivan, Arthur, 144
Swan, Owen, 29

Tanner, Robert, 31
Tate, Nahum, 82, 83, 85, 148
taverns, 24, 29, 113
Temperley, Nicholas, 157
Tempest, Thomas, 24
Temple Church, 43–4
Temple, Richard, 82
theatre music, 85–6
Theatre Royal, 37
Times, The, 149–51